REVOLT/COMPASSION

—

Six Scripts for
Contemporary Performance

Guernica Editions Inc. acknowledges the support
of the Canada Council for the Arts and the Ontario Arts Council.
The Ontario Arts Council is an agency of the Government of Ontario.
We acknowledge the financial support of the Government of Canada.

MICHAEL SPRINGATE

REVOLT/COMPASSION

Six Scripts for
Contemporary Performance

GUERNICA
EDITIONS

TORONTO • BUFFALO • LANCASTER (U.K.)
2019

Michael Mirolla, editor
Interior and cover design: Rafael Chimicatti
Guernica Editions Inc.
1569 Heritage Way, Oakville, (ON), Canada L6M 2Z7
2250 Military Road, Tonawanda, N.Y. 14150-6000 U.S.A.
www.guernicaeditions.com

Distributors:
University of Toronto Press Distribution,
5201 Dufferin Street, Toronto (ON), Canada M3H 5T8
Gazelle Book Services, White Cross Mills
High Town, Lancaster LA1 4XS U.K.

First edition.
Printed in Canada.

Legal Deposit—First Quarter
Library of Congress Catalog Card Number: 2018964199
Library and Archives Canada Cataloguing in Publication
Springate, Michael, 1952-
[Plays. Selections]
Revolt/compassion : six scripts for contemporary performance / Michael
Springate.

(Essential drama series ; 37)
Plays.
Issued in print and electronic formats.
ISBN 978-1-77183-396-7 (softcover).--ISBN 978-1-77183-397-4 (EPUB).--
ISBN 978-1-77183-398-1 (Kindle)

I. Title. II. Title: Six scripts for contemporary performance.

PS8587.P74A6 2019   C812'.54   C2018-906500-1
                                              C2018-906501-X

This collection is dedicated to Don Kugler, with thanks.

The difficulty, my friends, is not in avoiding death,
but in avoiding unrighteousness;
for that runs deeper than death.
— Socrates

CONTENTS

INTRODUCTION

THE FIRST PRESS-MENTION of Michael Springate is a 1971 *Globe and Mail* profile of Anglophones in Quebec City. Springate is identified as "the most articulate socialist" of the group of young people, whose on-going access to Quebecois culture and leftist politics distinguish them from the middle-aged cohort of interviewees. His interest in language, culture, and progressive politics remain and are on view in this collection. But as important in this sketch is the particular perspective that having Quebec roots has afforded him.

As a member of a linguistic minority within a minority-language province that borders the United States, Springate explores the vantage point of the non-dominant, secondary, or simply atypical player whose very position on the sidelines of the main event grants them insight into the workings of domination. Perched beside an English-speaking world power yet partially insulated from it thanks to the French language and Quebec's cultural protectionism, Quebec Anglophones occupy a kind of insider-outsider position with respect to francophone Quebec, to a predominantly Anglophone Canada, and to the United States. And Springate has paid particular attention to the workings of History, its drivers, clashes, and outcomes, from his second-row seat. Small nations and second-tier states recur in his oeuvre – Ukraine, Korea, Quebec – where their non-dominant relations to grand historical narratives are presented with insight and sympathy.

As a speaker of two languages and an apprentice to a range of others, Springate also believes that language is a profoundly social phenomenon – populations agree over time through various kinds of learning and in different circumstances on common understandings and usages of words. This openness of language to reformulation, its elaboration through usage is, of course, one of the riches of linguistic expression, especially for creative writers. Listen to how The American Friend of *Küt* interrogates the warring meanings of "innocence" and "guilt" in relation to "strategy" and "design" in a time of war, for instance:

> *It used to bother me that I had killed the innocent*
> *as well as the guilty. It doesn't bother me anymore.*
> *Not that. I've thought more deeply about it. It's only*
> *a conceit to pretend that there's a real distinction. [...]*
> *It's our strategic goals which determine guilt*
> *or innocence. It took me a while to understand that.*

As the example of *Küt* also shows, the power of language to reify can lead to profound misunderstandings of the situation being discussed, and cause great harm and alienation.

The gulf between the idea and its linguistic expression is represented in *Historical Bliss*, when the Man cannot make his actions match the verbal directions provided him. The reifying potency of words is examined in *Dog and Crow* through the demagoguery of Italy's fascist leader, Benito Mussolini; for instance, when his mistress, Claretta Petacci, urges him to tear up the 1939 Pact of Friendship and Alliance between Germany and Italy, insisting: "It's only words," he replies:

> *It isn't words. No! Not delicate ink stains.*
> *Geography! Land! If you can read the map*
> *you can read the future. There's a straight line*
> *between Berlin and Rome and around this Axis*
> *the continent spins.*

He confuses, willingly, the model for the reality – the map for the territory. In *Freeport, Texas*, the danger of misrecognizing how language works is laid bare at a more intimate level: A young woman's discourse concerning independence becomes an obstacle to her self-understanding; here, language alienates her from her own experience and sense of self.

Springate contends: "All good theatre is anti-language, and works hard to fight the reification at which language excels." And so, in his creative practice Springate has seemed to follow two connected paths: a rigorous pursuit of the expressive potentials and pitfalls of linguistic expression, and a turn to other arts for their ways of navigating the movement from idea or concept to its full expression. In these integrated, simultaneous efforts, Springate's oeuvre queries the roots of theatre, innovates at the level of form, and offers clear purposes for this performing art.

Language

Each of the pieces in this volume are "writerly" plays. Intentionally fashioned, precise in their diction, and allusive in their references, these plays ask for the reader's collaboration. Readers are not simple receivers of the scripts' pre-determined or encoded meanings; rather, they must find their way in, are encouraged to change perspective, and participate in the interpretation of the text. In large part because of Springate's consciously crafted use of language, when reading his history plays, I have the sense of time expanding. These six scripts for contemporary performance command my full attention. Their poetry – by which I mean the considered arrangement of the words, the shape of the text on the page, the accretion of meaning across the play, its solicitation of the reader's increased awareness – activates the senses without necessarily dictating where they should take me or what I should make of them. I listen for cadence and resonance and other shapes of sound. The images they conjure and the sensations they effect slow time through a process of immersion. I'm in.

At the same time, the ideas unfolded through these plays require a different vantage, a theoretical engagement. How can we locate ourselves in history? Where do art and politics intersect? What can words convey? How does social change come about? What part of memory and ideology is imagination? Revolt and compassion – are these stances toward the world in contradiction with each other, or a contradiction with which to begin? Such questions move us toward philosophy, toward engaging fundamental questions of existence, morality, societal organisation, human significance. Here too, I'm in.

Moving between experience and concept, event and reflection, my reading positions me at once as actor and chorus in a Greek tragedy – I am the maker of choices as well as the presenter of principle. Springate captures this tension in the image of eyes and forehead. In *Historical Bliss*, the first of the six scripts for contemporary performance gathered in this collection, a voice-over narrates an act of reading as follows:

> *There was an article I read recently.*
> *It was about a war economy.*
> *I read it quietly, slowly, occasionally looking at myself*
> *in the window beside my desk. At night, the window*
> *acts as mirror, dimly, the eyes are in shadow*
> *and only the forehead is clear.*

I mention my experience of reading Springate's plays – and that of the *Historical Bliss* narrator – because they signal a key aspect of his project as I understand it: His plays offer the reader a felt sense of time and of tense. He thus explores and capitalizes on a fundament of theatre as an art form, that it is an art of the present tense: As an event, it happens; as a representation it makes present. As he puts it: "Theatre is an act of relationship that brings us to the present tense, that shows choice." That is, theatre is not simply an artistic medium nor a mode for telling stories, though it is also those things. Indeed, all of his plays thematise relationship. Some are about familial or otherwise intimate relationships – of wives and husbands who do not share the same worldview (most starkly in the marriage of Dorothy and Ezra Pound in *Dog and Crow*), of children and parents (trying to bridge death [*Kareena*] and belief [*Küt*]), of fellow war-veterans (in *Küt*). Some excavate relationships to the world – *The Consolation of Philosophy* follows Orpheus into Hades to explore idealism and materialism, while The Man in

Historical Bliss struggles to locate himself in layers of performance. Most engage the relationship of societies and political systems to each other, and to their underlying principles (East and the West, fascism and communism, Christianity and Confucianism).

To return to Springate's description of theatre above, theatre is also an *act* of relation. The scripts collected here privilege the verbal act of relation – dialogue – both formally and in their content. This is perhaps most immediately apparent in the three dramas – *Dog and Crow* (1987), *Kareena* (2000), and *Freeport, Texas* (2004) – where many scenes are extended debates, often between two characters with starkly opposed perceptions. In *Freeport, Texas*, for instance, a Russian economist disputes self-serving, capitalist notions of freedom with an American corporate president and his daughter. The distinction between freedom *from* and freedom *to* undergirds a lovers' discussion about commitment in *Kareena*. *Dog and Crow* is replete with scenes of ideological jousting and seduction (sometimes these are the same thing).

His theatre acts relation at the level of structure as well. The sonata form, in which a major and minor musical theme are introduced, developed and recapitulated in relation to each other, has proven "a simple but highly effective way to organize thematic materials without recourse to a plot," he avers. In this collection, this musical structure that expands on two themes notably organises the two solo-performance works: *Historical Bliss* (1983) and *Küt: Shock and Awe* (2006). The first exhibits a binary structure that moves between the "Voice" and the "Man." The second – which is also the most recent of his scripts – progresses in a series of counterpointed motifs. This foundation upholds the plays' characterological examinations of split voices or psyches, as well as their thematic investigations of human perspective-change – which is to say, perhaps, transformation. In theory of language, as we've seen, the line from idea to word is not divinely directed, straight, nor unidirectional. In *Historical Bliss* and *Küt*, this insight is applied to subjectivity, or character, which is, in his words, "a composite of experience and intention." The relation these forms of incident and reflection take is also an action – not a given. Herein lies the hope for change.

Languages of the Stage

Springate's is a *théâtre de recherche*. It is research-driven and emerges in tandem with a research framework and practice. That is, his theatre works are part and parcel of a systematic study of an issue or phenomenon; they are a means to explore and enrich research questions and a way of sharing them with the public. His work is born out of overlapping areas of research into, among many other things: world dramatic literature (note the influences of Japanese Noh drama in *Dog and Crow*, for instance); dominant, residual, and emergent socio-political formations; cross-cultural encounter and relation; and other arts that provide additional "languages of the stage."

Sometimes those issues or phenomena are social or political, as in the case of *Freeport, Texas*, where "the realities of deregulated American industry merge with the after-effects of the Cold War." Always, it seems to me, the issues or phenomena are artistic. How can theatre work like film? Does a physical or choreographic "text" illuminate or reconfigure a written one? Can dramatic narrative be reorganised according to musical principles? Such allied arts are plumbed in Springate's creative process and in his pieces for their non-literary structures, their ways of moving from idea to instantiation, and from point *a* to point *b* in a narrative. This interdisciplinarity is a defining feature of his career.

This principle of always at least two (two voices, two arts, two themes) informs his creations from the 1970s to today. Introduced to theatre by his sister, Wendy Springate, and having performed in productions at McGill's Players' Theatre (including a W.B. Yeats play) in the year he was a student there, Springate made his first mark in professional theatre in his native Quebec City in 1971, when he and Grant Mathieu co-founded the Quebec City Summer Stock Theatre. This company of young people mounted a season of summer stock for the small Anglophone population of the city (6% of the population) and the thousands of Canadian and American tourists who visited the capitol.

But a diet of Anglo-American comedies, however appreciative the audience, was not sustaining, particularly for an artist influenced by the experimental, image-forward processes and productions of Montreal's Théâtre expérimental des femmes and Carbone 14 (with whom he would later collaborate on *Opium*, 1987). While a student of painting and drawing at the Montreal Museum School of Fine Arts, he founds the experimental Painted Bird Theatre (1974-1984), an interdisciplinary, ensemble company of actors, visual artists, musicians, and dancers which, as its name implies, stood out from its theatrical surroundings.

In an era of nationalist and social realist playwriting in Quebec in both English and French, and an English-language theatre scene dominated by the fairly conservative institutional theatre – the Centaur theatre and the Saidye Bronfman Centre theatre, this inter-artistic collective shared a space and some performers for a time with Powerhouse Gallery (now La Centrale), a feminist, artist-run space that incubated early performance art by Tanya Mars, among others.

With the likes of Wendy Springate, Diane Morrison, Jacky Bouchard, Joanne Gormley, Jan Pottie, Martin Kevan, Graham Chartier, Ari Snyder, and Jaroslaw Hirniak, Painted Bird staged creations that experimented with non-literary dramaturgical structures that allowed for a certain level of abstraction. For instance, the organisational principle for *Improvisation in Sonata Form I* (1979) was "movements," each of which had a particular tempo to which the onstage sculptor, piano player, and two actors had to adhere in their discipline-based improvisations. *Twelve Tones* (1980) used musical composition as a structural and metaphorical element to braid "themes of indifference, randomness, violence, and exploitation." But sound as the place from which textual interpretation for performance begins was equally evident in their 1976 production of Beckett's *Endgame*, according to theatre critic, Keith Garebian, who had also reviewed *Twelve Tones*.

Indeed, Painted Bird was lauded by the *Montreal Star* theatre critic, Myron Galloway, for its imaginative, smartly paced, and compellingly acted stagings of morally complex dramas by the likes of Beckett, Buchner, and Stoppard. Painted Bird's early *Fugue* (1977) similarly brought musical and textual structure together in its interlacing of Yeat's *Purgatory*, Mishima's *The Lady Aoi*, and Springate's own *In the Possession*, each of which features a protagonist with a split consciousness.

When he subsequently took on the mantle of Artistic Director of Playwrights' Workshop Montreal in 1984, investigation of sound-text relations continued in his New Text – New Music program, under the direction of Montreal librettist and playwright, Don Druick. And as Artistic Director of Prairie Theatre Exchange in Winnipeg (1988-1992) and the Factory Theatre in Toronto, his commitment to innovative new plays manifested itself in original productions of Margaret Sweatman, Connie Gault, Carol Shields, Tom Walmsley, Bill Harrar, and Andrew Moody among others, as well as a remount of his own *Dog and Crow* in a production openly influenced by Felix Mirbt's puppetry work – including the use of actor-manipulators of large-scale puppets – in Montreal.

Unsurprisingly then, Springate's sustained creative research into the arts' different relations to temporality, image, and representation is evident in this collection too. For instance, both of his solo plays – *Historical Bliss* and *Küt: Shock and Awe* – are shaped in the time-structures and modalities of other forms: film and Korean p'ansori, respectively. Indeed, *Küt* is a multi-media piece for an actor who plays all the roles and a musician which, in its first performance in 2006, included film sequences created by Carolyn Combs. *The Consolation of Philosophy* is an oratorio composed for solo voices (including ten, first-person sonnets) and chorus; interleaved between such contemplative and epic segments is a dialogic argument about the foundation of reality between the late Roman writer, Boethius, and a personified Lady Philosophy. *Dog and Crow*, which dissects what Springate calls "an angry but ascendant modernism – represented by Ezra Pound and Benito Mussolini," alludes in substance and style to Pound's writings, of which *Dog and Crow* ends up clearly critical.

Contradiction and a Place to Begin

> *I imagined a chorus which said*
> *that consolation is not possible,*
> *unless on the path of compassion,*
> *unless on the road of revolt.*

In the fifth and final book of Michael Springate's *The Consolation of Philosophy*, the early medieval philosopher Boethius speaks the words above to Lady Philosophy. This is the book in which true dialogue is achieved on a set of crucial human questions; books one to four announce one or the other character "writ[ing]," "convers[ing] with," "recount[ing]," and "tr[ying] to talk to." Four attempts, four sequences in which the pair elliptically work from their contradictory perspectives toward consolation. Faced with the suffering of the children huddled together in hunger and cold at Boethius's feet in the ten opening sonnets and who are the subject of his first conversation with Lady Philosophy in Book Two, they finally *Try And Succeed To Speak Together* in the oratorio's final book.

In unison, they assert the worthiness of the non-dominant:

> *For we and our children*
> *are not unworthy of life,*
> *our poverty the proof.*

Through this common foundation, born of need, one division is bridged: "your children" from Book Two have become "our children" in Book Five. The contradiction in the philosophers' points of view too resolves – not as a singular destination, but as a mutual point of departure: "The path well travelled becomes the road. / Compassion to revolt is a question of use."

Always at least two, as the place to begin. Again.

Erin Hurley, McGill University
3 September 2018

HISTORICAL BLISS

A Japanese woman appears dressed in a beautiful gold and black kimono: face and hands whitened, small red mouth, loose hair falling below the shoulder. She stands very still, eyes closed, in the corner of a very simple almost empty room.

In a very understated, calm and slow-moving fashion she follows the instructions of the male voice-over. The voice is soft, coaxing, but insistent.

VOICE: O.K. Open your eyes.
      Slowly, slowly, as if you were thinking.
      Now lean forward, just slightly.
      You're balancing against the wind.
      Good. Good.

      Small steps.
      The heel of one foot to the instep
      of the other. Fine.

      You're on a field at dawn.
      Walking against the wind.
      Mauve. It's all mauve about you.

      Keep coming. That's it.
      Lean. Lean.

      O.K. Now stop.
      Look about you, slowly, slowly.
      Change direction.
      Hesitate.
      Now you're sure.
      Small steps.

      The heel of one foot to the instep
      of the other.

      Lean. Slowly. Hesitate. Slowly.
      Head up. Please, head up.
      Good. Good. Very good.

You can hear the wind.
You can see distances.

*She stands serenely, as if listening for a distant sound. She slowly
raises her hands to shift her hair to one side, letting it fall in front
of one shoulder where she gently combs it with her fingers.*

Films, I would say, the voice of the people,
I would say, celluloid heaven, I would say,
films, how the camera moves and the subject
is lit, edited, and you, I would say, you,
dressed as a geisha and serving tea,
a subject, I would think, to be lit, to be edited.
But you stammered, " this is the cleanest thing,
the cleanest thing I've ever done."
You stammered, while I can only repeat.

Precisely this private ritual, serving tea
at certain moments which you chose,
I don't know why but I enjoyed it,
reminded me of a film. You said your father
you didn't know, only your mother, two sisters,
a brother, living in institutional green mudflats
which you left at fourteen.
⠀⠀⠀⠀⠀⠀Our blessed St. Catherine,
our bitter St. Lawrence, and where they cross,
some tricks, all johns, and then you said never again,
I will work at the fast food donut-coffee stands
at Alexis Nihon Plaza. You told me all that
one particular evening while removing the white
after … having appeared. Not knowing what to do
⠀⠀⠀⠀⠀⠀⠀⠀I talked about films,
slightly, no, very uncomfortable, I talked about films.

I would like to film you I said
and you said nothing.

She turns to cross to the tea-tray with handmade teapot and teabowl on it.

> I would like to film history, I said,
> how oral cultures personify history
> through spirits from the past and you,
> I would say, are a spirit,
>   let me film history
> and you said nothing,
>
> But why don't you listen, I said,
> don't you understand, it all makes sense,
> it all makes sense I said, grasping at straws,
>   the subject lit
> before you remove the white.

She kneels. With sustained movements she explores the tea implements as the voice grows ever more insistent, harassed.

> In the film, there's this shot of a woman at the foot
> of the stairs, this is how I told you, a shot of the
> woman at the foot of the stairs who is wearing
> glasses, then the camera cuts away and returns
> quickly, the glasses are broken, smashed, she's been
> shot in the eye—well, you can assume she's been
> shot in the eye, something's happened to her eye.
> You should see it, I said, montage, also a crowd
> scene, must be hundreds of extras, thousands of
> them, must have cost a fortune, and the people
> are running down the steps after being fired upon
> by the Cossacks who are wearing these really
> beautiful, colourful, colourful costumes—well,
> the film is in black and white but you can tell that
> the costumes must be colourful, I mean you can
> tell that they must have put thousands of dollars
> of detail into it, anyway, the Cossacks are wearing

these beautiful colourful costumes in black and
white and the crowd is this total chaos moving
from the left to the right, I mean, the left side of
the screen to the right, and juxtaposed to all this
is a woman, carrying the body of her dead child,
carrying from right to left and the sense of weight,
of force, just in the simple fact of having her move
in a simple, orderly, and opposite direction from
the streaming chaos of the previous shots, I mean,
its absolutely incredible, and the sense of chaos,
not through a lot if you really look, not through
a lot, but just different perspective, not a lot but
different, and the lions, there's this amazing thing
with stone sculptures, lions, one lying, one rising,
one standing, in sequence, and it's a powerful rage
of stone, a stone lion standing up and the castle
walls tumbling down, tumbling down, the Tsar
tumbling down, the chaos, not through a lot if you
really look, but the different perspective on a few
all cut up and juggled for effect, you should see it,
each shot set up like a still, only it moves, along,
stills that move, you understand, moving stills,
it's film, it's absolutely film, Potemkin, it's called
Potemkin, the film is named after the mutiny, after
the mutiny …

I was saying, I was going to say,
and it was then that you smashed the bowl,
you smashed it against the floor.

She raises the teabowl to her lips.

I was quiet, you were serene.
Clay fragments on tile.

She drinks.

> You can't do it right until you get a feeling
> for the violence underneath,
> was all you said—later.

She stands and begins to slowly remove kimono, wig, revealing a man with receding hairline.

> You, a Polish Jew raised on St. Lawrence Street,
> serving tea in a Japanese kimono and whiteface.

> Later, as you left me, I asked, I asked you in anger:
> "Do you choose fantasy over politics because
> you're ignorant, or because you haven't the guts to
> tell the difference?"

He moves to a small table beside a window where he removes the make-up, washes.

> There was an article I read recently.
> It was about a war economy.
> I read it quietly, slowly, occasionally looking at myself
> in the window beside my desk. At night, the window
> acts as mirror, dimly, the eyes are in shadow
> and only the forehead is clear.
> I enjoy articles which are well documented,
> where one can check the translations
> of original references. I reread the article,
> quickly this time; other articles, too,
> other publications about economic structure,
> war, socialization of the individual.
> I thought about you, and our child.
> I thought about my loneliness, after you left.
> I thought in silence.

> Perhaps a certain direction is maintained
> by thinking in silence.

Perhaps not. Perhaps not.

Am I grasping at straws? Yes, to focus perhaps,
on the hands, perhaps, on the space as it is carved
by the hands, perhaps, on the surface, as it is worked.

Words focus, but what words are left?
Words themselves can focus
        on the words themselves
            but then the eyes are in shadow
and only the forehead is clear.

It is night when one looks to the window
and sees only one's reflection.

Are there things that can be done?

He moves away from the table and sits, head in hands.

    Head up, please, head up.
    We'll begin again, starting at the beginning,
    but this time clumsy movements, falling,
    exaggeration,—don't worry, it will come naturally.

    O.K. Open your eyes.

His eyes spring open

    Slowly, slowly.
    As if you were thinking.

    Now lean forward, just slightly.

He leans forward precariously.

    You're balancing against the wind.
    Good. Good. Uh, I think
    this would be better if you stood.

He stands.

> Right. Now lean again,
> against the wind …

He licks a finger and raises it to find the direction of the wind.

> Uh, it's a metaphor. The wind,
> it's only a metaphor.
> Just lean.
>
> Now, small steps.

He doesn't appear to move.

> Are you moving?

He nods his head assertively.

> Well, take noticeably small steps.
> The heel of one foot to the instep
> of the other.
>
> You're walking on a field at dawn.
> You're struggling against the metaphor.
> Mauve, it's all mauve about you.

He looks about himself incredulously.

> Keep coming. That's it.
> Good. Good. Very good.

Once again it appears that he is not moving.

> Noticeably small. Very good. Very subtle.
> Um, not too subtle, you have to do something.
> *Noticeably* small, *noticeably* subtle.

He falls forward.

> That's better. They'll see that one.
> O.K. Now stop.

He freezes mid-step.

> Uh, finish the step first.
>
> Now, stop. Look about you.
> Slowly! Slowly!
> Change direction.
> Hesitate. Now you're sure.
> Small steps. Hesitate. Change direction.
> Lean. Stop. As at the beginning. Finish.
> Slowly. Noticeably. Noticeably subtle.
> Change. With confidence, my God,
> with some confidence!
> Good. Good. Very good.

He smiles hopefully, his body hopelessly contorted.

> You can hear the wind.
> You can see distances.

The absurdity of the situation dawns upon him and the voice simultaneously.

> Perhaps not.
> Perhaps not.

The actor begins to speak. It is clear that it has been his recorded voice all along.

ACTOR: Next sequence, patterns of saturated colour
           framed on the darkening street crowded thoroughfare.

A suspended shot of baroque wrought iron.
A woman and child's reflection glides by
in a store window. A man stumbles. A man runs.
Next sequence, a hand held camera captures
his profile slightly facing up, eyes closing.
He is surrounded by the shining and barking
> of the marketplace.
>> He tries to remember
>> how to speak.

Next sequence, him, bent double,
a strange noise echoing from his body.
Con tract, Con *tract*.
Con tract, Con *tract*.

Next sequence, a man on the street his vision
filled with the saturated colours of night.

Next sequence, a man trying to remember
how to speak.

Next sequence, *con* tract, con *tract*.

Next sequence, an image of one's memories
made visible.

He kneels, as at a tea ceremony, and breaks the bowl.

Tentative next sequence, voices singing.

He sings, the tune suggestive of a missing harmony.

> Dogs eat dogs and the whales sing
> A song is a song if sight it brings
> Sing a song of sixpence pocket full of lies
> The lives in the middle live in my eye
> And there's a whining in the distance
> In the distance

Dogs eat dogs and the whales die
Sing a song of sorrow an evening sky
Who sang that song as they blinded our eyes
Now there's a barking in the distance
In the distance

He stops singing. Rises.

Next sequence: and I await the return of her
or the voice of her of who can say who
entered whom upon the floor covered with sweat
the light through venetian blinds as headlights
sweep the ceiling all those who

flattened shadows crawl seeking food
shadows seeking crevices flattened crawl
seeking food

sand in mouths sand in eyes discussing sand
my tongue against yours swift reptilian splendour
in headlights well dressed edited crowds
old factory experimental film house old house
prosperous whore house windows are sheathed
in hand painted advertisements encrusted
steel bars

many, many mouths whitened, eyes blackened,
mouths blackened, eyes whitened slow turquoise
humming arm glistens neon sweat carves surface
worked

headlights, strata, strata

face on scaffold imprint hands on stairs ascending
two shot voice from room razored light clock
clock clock and I and I or it in silent swan lengths
along the muscled back above the swelling

swollen summer night moon presses against the dawn
pan and fade I see you within the field with little child
little one hold my hand this curb careful
successful crossing

canyons of banking dread banking dread making
that not inevitable inevitable close-up face
wincing and I await the brushed sky healing ochre,
pale green, throats of blue, dawn, strata,
celluloid, moss

traces of ever so light garnet moss on cracked
concrete seen beyond the goldfish cut-outs on
the desk as the camera pulls back to the sleeping
form, we quote the quotes and rediscover context
in the contrapuntal shadows emerging brow the
eyes flicker, perhaps, yes, there it is, would you like
me to turn slightly and then the line or just hold
the pose, hold the pose? all right, softer, "a walk,
I just went for a walk, no I didn't see anybody, it's
easy to walk for a long time, what are you doing
awake?" should I cross here? O.K. I'll try with an
arm against the wall, a touch peeved, you know,
the silence being broken, "I didn't mean to wake
you, I was just waiting, sort of, I don't know what
for I was just waiting, looking out the window."
rubbing the forehead is a bit obvious what if I just
twist one wrist with the other hand? make it more
demanding, ask the question, "I didn't mean to
wake you, I was just waiting sort of, I don't know
what for I was just waiting looking out the window,
yeah, I didn't expect to, things on my mind, no, it's
not you, just thoughts, is the little one asleep? Did
she? That's good." I could laugh, we could share a
moment of quiet laughter, "Is the little one asleep?
Did she? That's good. It's great." that's better, beside
the bed, softly, "Do you want to hear a story?" no,

no stories, just a silence on my heels beside her as
she breathes, the gaze moving about the room with
a steady persistence, next shot, new scene, she's
singing slightly in the late afternoon, I'm reading
the lens filled with a tight scrawl, I interrupt and
read out-loud she continues singing next shot,
just the woman and the voice of the child next
shot same scene through the eyes of the child the
camera is always angled up the sound is large and
garbled the faces swim into focus next shot the
hands of the man tearing at his face next shot the
man alone shown only by the shadow still on the
screen perhaps paralyzed on the screen discussing
history to the back of a woman slowly turning
next shot no shot the film is ended the man alone
not even a shadow screaming into the dawn that
certain things need not be so, that is

The actor ceases speaking, the voice over begins.

VOICE: Next shot, a man in a room, alone,
             after the end of the film,
             stumbles upon his ideas of necessity
             changing, that is,
             hold my hand little one, careful,
             curb crossing, fixed thoughts splintering
             a rainbow arch on pavement.
             Next shot, a man in a room,
             after the end of the film
             after the end of the film
             peering through necessity
             stumbles upon the thing in itself changing,
             that is, hold my hand little one:
             value, judgment, decisions
             are reflective of social relations
             reflected in the individual

mediating proportionally,
earlier intentions a painted rainbow
on asphalt, next shot, a man in a room,
after the end of the film
after the end of the film
after the end of the film.

ACTOR:

As he speaks he tentatively performs the actions.

It is perhaps dawn, perhaps dusk.
The heel of one foot
to the instep of the other.
Lean. Head up.
The wind. The distance.

DOG AND CROW

CAST

EZRA POUND: American poet and translator
DOROTHY POUND: British wife of Ezra
ANTONIO: Peasant from Southern Italy
GRAZIA: Communist organizer
BENITO MUSSOLINI: Italian politician and dictator
CLARETTA PETACCI: Mistress and friend of Mussolini
INTERROGATOR FOR THE ITALIAN GOVERNMENT
PIETRO: Antonio's older brother
DR. OVERHOLSER: American psychiatrist
YOUNG MAN: Antonio's son, immigrant to US

SCENE ONE

A railway station, Italy, early 1930s. A man is barking. A woman stops to watch.

GRAZIA: What are you doing?

ANTONIO: I'm barking.

GRAZIA: I know that! Why?

ANTONIO: To show that it's not natural, that I'm not a dog.

GRAZIA: I thought maybe you wanted me to throw you some spare change, a few pennies to watch a man grovel.

ANTONIO: I don't beg.

GRAZIA: A dog that barks and doesn't beg?

ANTONIO: I'm not a dog.

GRAZIA: Are you practicing to become one? Or perhaps you want to show the public that you're crazy.

ANTONIO: If they think a man barking is crazy, then they are asleep. So now I have two reasons to bark, first I should wake the public, and second …

He wavers in his thoughts, distracted.

GRAZIA: When was the last time you ate?

Ezra and Dorothy are seen passing to catch a train.

ANTONIO: I am dizzy because I am standing at a great height, far below me, catching trains, wearing hats, kissing … You ask why I bark, for the price of a meal I'll tell you. Buy me a meal and I'll tell you why I bark.

SCENE TWO

On the train.

EZRA: *Morte gentil, rimedio d'cattivi*
Merze merze, a man glunte ti chieggo,
Viemmi a veder, o prendimi, che peggio
Mi face Amor che miei spiriti vivi.

I'm having trouble translating this one. It's meaning
resides in the intangibles.

DOROTHY: Why do you say that?

EZRA: The words are simple, simple enough, but the voice
which places them just so, inflects them just so,
makes them cohere ... That's the hard part, making
it cohere.

DOROTHY: The landscape is so beautiful, an horizon gently
appearing, gently disappearing.

EZRA: It doesn't so much elude me as ...
perhaps it eludes me.

DOROTHY: What eludes you?

EZRA: His intentions. His intentions elude me.

DOROTHY: Don't stop reading. I enjoy it.

EZRA: *Son consumati e spenti si che quivi,*
Dov'io staba gioiso, pra m'avveggio
In parte lasso la dov'io possegui
Pene e dolor, e'n pianto vuol ch'arrivi,

E molto maggior mal, s'esser piu puote.
Morte, or e il tempo, che valer mi puoi
Di tormi da le man di tal nimico.

Aime lasso, quante volte dico:
Amor, perche fai mal sol pure a'tuoi,

Com'fa quel de l'inferno, che percuote?

Overlap into scene three.

SCENE THREE

Antonio and Grazia in a small crowded cafe.

ANTONIO: If it was my cafe I wouldn't serve us. I certainly
            wouldn't serve me. Not unless we showed our
            money first.

GRAZIA: I know the cook.

ANTONIO: It helps, it helps.

GRAZIA: Have you ever read this?

ANTONIO: It's a newspaper.

GRAZIA: Have you ever read it?

ANTONIO: I don't think so.

GRAZIA: Can you read?

ANTONIO: Slowly, very slowly.

GRAZIA: What do you do?

ANTONIO: I'm learning Latin.

GRAZIA: How are you learning Latin if you can't read?

ANTONIO: I look at the words carved in the buildings. I look at
            the letters, then I ask the people who pass by what
            the words mean. That is how I am learning Latin.

GRAZIA: Do you work?

ANTONIO: Soon, soon.

GRAZIA: Soon?

ANTONIO: I left the South two years ago. After a while I found
           a job at Fiat. My wife and child still live in the
           South, I send them money.

GRAZIA: Recently? Have you sent them money recently?

ANTONIO: Soon. You'll see. I'll find something

GRAZIA: Were you fired?

ANTONIO: Why are you asking all these questions?

GRAZIA: It's not a lot of questions.

ANTONIO: They serve us food. You say it's because you know
           the cook. How do you know the cook?

GRAZIA: We work together.

ANTONIO: Doing what?

GRAZIA: Political work.

ANTONIO: What does that mean?

GRAZIA: We belong to the same party.

ANTONIO: A secret party?

GRAZIA: Illegal, not secret. There's a difference.

ANTONIO: I understand. You have secret meetings to discuss
           how not to get caught at secret meetings.

GRAZIA: Exactly.

ANTONIO: You print a newspaper?

GRAZIA: Yes.

ANTONIO: You don't believe in what we're told?

GRAZIA: Do you?

ANTONIO:	I don't know. I try to sniff out the truth.
GRAZIA:	Very scientific.
ANTONIO:	Why do I think your newspaper says the same thing over and over?
GRAZIA:	If the crimes are repeated the analysis should be also.
ANTONIO:	Nothing is going to change.
GRAZIA:	To those who hunt us nothing is changing. To those who need us we are getting stronger.
ANTONIO:	You're an idiot.
GRAZIA:	Then you won't help?
ANTONIO:	You haven't asked.
GRAZIA:	I'm asking.
ANTONIO:	What exactly do you want me to do?
GRAZIA:	Help in distribution.
ANTONIO:	Why should I help you?
GRAZIA:	The paper is printed in the country. It gets brought to a depot in the city which changes as often as we can. From there it has to be brought in small bundles to certain factories, churches, houses.
ANTONIO:	Cafes?
GRAZIA:	A few.
ANTONIO:	Why do you trust me?
GRAZIA:	You have nothing to lose, in our eyes that makes you valuable.
ANTONIO:	I have nothing to lose.

SCENE FOUR

Benito Mussolini and Ezra Pound, Rome 1933.

BENITO: I have been told that you are a distinguished man of letters, that your work has had international influence. It is a pleasure to meet you.

EZRA: It was kind of your cultural offices to arrange this interview.

BENITO: My offices indicate that you have played a significant role in the world of English writing.

EZRA: Perhaps I have some influence, these things are hard to say.

BENITO: It is always difficult to initiate change.

EZRA: It was less difficult when I was younger. I was more certain of success when I was less certain of what I was doing.

BENITO: You also translate?

EZRA: Yes.

BENITO: From Italian?

EZRA: Increasingly. I have just finished a translation of the complete works of Cavalcanti.

BENITO: The Renaissance.

EZRA: Early Renaissance.

BENITO: Yes. History will look on that period as only one of Italy's great accomplishments. Do you enjoy living here?

EZRA: I was born in the USA, emigrated to England, moved to France and settled in Italy. Some would call it a logical progression.

BENITO: You show a quick wit.

EZRA: I like plain talk.

BENITO: So do I. I consider it a virtue. You have asked to present a submission.

EZRA: There are a few matters of importance I have long wanted to bring to your attention. This is an eighteen-point memorandum outlining ideas on economic policy.

BENITO: So many, when discussing money matters, never consider the possibilities of will, a disciplined national will.

EZRA: That is why Italy is being so closely watched. You are not afraid to make changes. To choose.

BENITO: It's rare, isn't it, a government not afraid of governing? Strikes were crippling the country, we re-organized the unions. Why not? It was for the good of all. I believe in the good of all. We have made Italy internationally competitive, respected. We have created order from chaos. Not everyone accepts it. They prefer to hide behind concepts from the last century—bourgeois, proletariat. They don't realize that upon the ashes of the World War a new society is being built. We live in a very exciting time, Mr. Pound.

EZRA: I think your struggle quite comparable to that of the founding fathers of America. You remind me of President Jefferson, a man committed to sound economics as the basis of a lasting social order.

BENITO: It's not the first time I have heard that comparison. An editorial in *The New York Times* made a similar comment.

EZRA: I see you pay close attention to details.

BENITO: An editorial in *The New York Times* is not a detail. The foreign perception of Italy is important. For too long the English speaking world has perceived my country through British eyes. That is changing. Perhaps you noticed that it was your kind American ambassador who wrote the introduction to my autobiography.

EZRA: I had noticed.

BENITO: A generous introduction. Generous, but true. I was born poor. I am not ashamed of it. But here I now stand, head of my country, proof that change is possible.

EZRA: It's with faith in change that I offer this memorandum.

BENITO: When time permits I will consider it carefully.

EZRA: I have brought something else, a draft of thirty cantos, the beginning of my major work as a poet, I would be honoured if you would accept this copy.

BENITO: Tell me, how is it that a recognized man of letters is so concerned with economics?

EZRA: Aren't they related? Isn't it all a part of a man putting his thoughts in order?

BENITO: And why should a man put his thoughts in order?

EZRA: Isn't it the responsibility of those who are capable of it?

BENITO: Do you often answer one question with another?

EZRA: Yes.

BENITO: Then permit me one in return. These poems of
          yours, are they written to stir the enthusiasms of
          the people?

EZRA: I don't write for those who despair.

BENITO: Entertaining. A very entertaining distinction. Not
          for those who despair.

EZRA: I think writing should be useful.

BENITO: Yes, so do I. Useful. I'm glad to receive your works.
          I hope you will continue to correspond with our
          cultural offices. Exchanges such as these can only
          increase understanding between our peoples.

EZRA: Perhaps we could correspond directly, there are so
          many thoughts ...

BENITO: If you wish ... of course. My door is always open.

EZRA: I appreciate, I do appreciate your time.

Exit Ezra Pound. Enter Claretta Petacci.

CLARETTA: Are all your conversations so boring?

BENITO: Most of them. It was kind of you not to enter
          before it was over.

CLARETTA: You said I could use your private entrance.

BENITO: Did I say that?

CLARETTA: You enjoy being surprised. But you always say the
          same things in your interviews. Why?

BENITO: You don't know?

CLARETTA: I wouldn't have asked.

BENITO:	To succeed you don't need many thoughts, just a few infinitely repeated.
CLARETTA:	It's not the first time you've said that, either.
BENITO:	You asked. It helps, too, if you keep the ideas simple.
CLARETTA:	A disciplined national will.
BENITO:	Claretta, leave me alone. I'm working. This is a working day.
CLARETTA:	Are you angry I came in?
BENITO:	Have you ever seen me angry? Stern, perhaps, impassioned, moved, bitter, thunderous, but angry? Why should a man who has everything be angry?
CLARETTA:	That woman is outside again, the crazy one who claims that you are the father of her child.
BENITO:	Is she yelling?
CLARETTA:	She was. Now she's just standing quietly.
BENITO:	Tell my secretary to give her some money.
CLARETTA:	Not everything can be solved with money.
BENITO:	I'm sure she puts on a fascinating show. The money can come from the cultural budget.
CLARETTA:	He's an ugly child.
BENITO:	She brings it with her?
CLARETTA:	Him, she brings him with her.
BENITO:	If it's ugly it can't be mine.
CLARETTA:	Why not? She says she is not a whore but the mother of your child.

BENITO:	I don't know the woman. I never saw her before she started coming. There are many women who fantasize about important men. She is …
CLARETTA:	Insane?
BENITO:	Yes.
CLARETTA:	I believe you. She is insane. But still, she has her own feelings, her own world. Is there nothing we can do?
BENITO:	Let her go to church, to those blessed fathers who make a virtue out of ignorance and poverty.
CLARETTA:	Don't speak of the church like that.
BENITO:	Don't make me laugh. You don't believe in religion any more than I do.
CLARETTA:	They deserve respect.
BENITO:	For what? Their history of lies? Their long and noble history of lies? I went to a school run by the sacred fathers. At meal time we were separated into tables depending on the fees paid by our parents, and then we were fed; fed accordingly, according to the fees. I was fed the least. It made no difference who was hungry, only who paid what. Divine rule.
CLARETTA:	Benito, my little Benito.
BENITO:	Yes, there is something you can do for me.
CLARETTA:	What?
BENITO:	Faith, Claretta. You need more faith, in this world, this world.
CLARETTA:	What do you want, Benito?
BENITO:	Such beautiful eyes, skin.

CLARETTA: There's more in this world than your desires.

BENITO: Claretta, come back. I want you to rub my forehead. The dome needs polishing. Your touch is so good. Why are you with me, Claretta?

CLARETTA: I don't know.

BENITO: Why?

CLARETTA: I told my sister that you always keep a loaded gun in your pocket. She took it literally.

BENITO: That's not why.

CLARETTA: No.

BENITO: To be poor is to be humiliated, and to be with me isn't to be poor, is that it?

CLARETTA: Yet you try to humiliate me all the time.

BENITO: To find out why you stay.

SCENE FIVE

Antonio and Grazia at street corner.

ANTONIO: Fides, fides. So many building have the word fides on them.

GRAZIA: Where are the newspapers?

ANTONIO: Fides means trust, doesn't it?

GRAZIA: The papers …

ANTONIO: The banks in particular like that word. High up, cut in thick stone.

GRAZIA: Where are they?

ANTONIO:	Fides.
GRAZIA:	How can we make the delivery?
ANTONIO:	We can't.
GRAZIA:	What did you do with the papers?
ANTONIO:	I junked them.
GRAZIA:	Where? Where did you junk them.
ANTONIO:	In the sewer.
GRAZIA:	Which sewer?
ANTONIO:	The one closest to me at the time.
GRAZIA:	You have wonderful powers of observation.
ANTONIO:	I noticed I was being followed.
GRAZIA:	Those papers are printed through donations of those who don't have pennies to spare. People risk their lives to get the bundle into your hands and you junked them and now think it's funny.
ANTONIO:	I don't think it's funny. I don't think it's a tragedy either. They're not sacred.
GRAZIA:	People learn of the present situation, the present situation, they make decisions dependent on that knowledge. Their decisions count. They need our newspaper. Actions in the factory are coordinated by our newspaper.
ANTONIO:	Each issue says the same thing.
GRAZIA:	That's not true. I trusted you.
ANTONIO:	You said I was doing fine.
GRAZIA:	And now because you think you might have been followed, at the very first sign of …

ANTONIO: You remember you said I had nothing to lose. You were wrong. I have my head. I am not anxious to lose it.

GRAZIA: At the first sign of danger you squirm.

ANTONIO: The people in the streets have never seemed so happy. They are all waving flags and singing patriotic songs.

GRAZIA: People cling to what they know. They want to cling to what they know.

ANTONIO: And what they know is authority and what they want to know is success. Mussolini gives them both.

GRAZIA: The joys of a military victory in Africa will be short-lived, I promise you. Aerial bombardment of unarmed Ethiopians is not the resurrection of the Roman Empire. The people would interpret events differently if they had the right facts, the right analysis.

ANTONIO: That's why the newspaper.

GRAZIA: Bravo.

ANTONIO: Analysis.

GRAZIA: Yes.

ANTONIO: That's the word you use to pretend that the obvious doesn't exist.

GRAZIA: What's the obvious?

ANTONIO: Nothing we do makes any difference.

GRAZIA: Is that why you junked the newspapers?

ANTONIO: No.

GRAZIA: We do what we believe in.

ANTONIO:	Everybody says that.
GRAZIA:	I've made a terrible mistake.
ANTONIO:	Grazia, you can trust me.
GRAZIA:	Why? Why should I believe you?
ANTONIO:	I don't have to defend myself.
GRAZIA:	You no longer answer only to yourself.
ANTONIO:	Then who do I answer to? To you? I answer to myself and that's how it's going to stay.
GRAZIA:	I've made a terrible mistake.
ANTONIO:	No, you didn't. You haven't. You just don't understand what you're doing. You can trust me because I trust you, and if I didn't trust you then no amount of analysis would keep me here. I trust you, do you understand? I trust you.

SCENE SIX

Grazia and the Interrogator.

GRAZIA:	Why are the lights so bright?
INTER.:	Are they bright?
GRAZIA:	Yes.
INTER.:	We have nothing to hide. We don't mind bright lights. Our hands and rooms are clean.
GRAZIA:	I understand.
INTER.:	How do you make a living?
GRAZIA:	I don't.

INTER.:	You are, then, a parasite. Do you confess to being a parasite?
GRAZIA:	How do you make a living? Talking to parasites?
INTER.:	Finding them.
GRAZIA:	And then?
INTER.:	We think you are in contact with certain people we would like to find, certain people difficult to track down.
GRAZIA:	I don't understand.
INTER.:	Of course not. I haven't made myself clear.
GRAZIA:	Why am I arrested?
INTER.:	You are not arrested. This is a job interview. I am offering you a job.
GRAZIA:	I'd rather beg on street corners.
INTER.:	Lucrative?
GRAZIA:	Educational.
INTER.:	That's not where you get your money.
GRAZIA:	I don't understand.
INTER.:	Not yet. I don't expect you to understand yet. Have you seen this?
GRAZIA:	It's a newspaper.
INTER.:	Have you ever read it?
GRAZIA:	I can't read.
INTER.:	You can't read?
GRAZIA:	Well, I can, but slowly, slowly. By the time I get to the end of the sentence …

INTER.:   Tell me, what do you do with your time?

GRAZIA: I am trying to learn Latin. I look at the words
            carved in the buildings. I ask the people who pass
            by what they mean. So far I have learned that Fides
            means trust.

INTER.:   You get foreign funding for the paper, don't you?
            We know you're funded. We also know that you
            agitate within the factories.

GRAZIA: I have never felt comfortable at job interviews.

INTER.:   I have been asked to find out why certain factories
            continue to produce defective weapons. Sabotage?
            That at least is what your newspaper suggests. I
            think you can help me, and I know I can help you.
            You talk and I'll pay.

GRAZIA: You'll pay.

INTER.:   You understand.

GRAZIA: I don't think so.

INTER.:   This is a spoon, a small spoon. Very simple
            technology, a spoon. Simple design. It's easy to
            understand what to do with a spoon.

GRAZIA: It's good for soup.

INTER.:   We agree. It's good for soup. A spoon isn't good for
            cutting, is it? I mean, it's not very sharp. And it's too
            small to hit you with. If I wanted to cut you or beat
            you I wouldn't use a spoon, would I? What can I do
            with a spoon? I can balance an egg on it. It's well
            designed for that. Or an eye. I could balance an eye
            on it. If you talk … perhaps then I could put the
            spoon away. Such a small spoon, just slip it into my
            pocket. Right now I am going to relax and listen.
            You can give the names I seek, the information I

want, or you can be silent … In which case, after a certain pause, I am going to take out one of your eyes. And if you stay silent, I'll fill the spoon again. You shouldn't be frightened. If you really are a beggar then being blind can only help business, and if you aren't a beggar and yet tell me what I want to know then I will pay you for your troubles. You see, in my own way, I am anxious to help the poor, to help the poor help themselves.

GRAZIA: I understand.

INTER.: Good.

GRAZIA: You are hungry and want to eat my eyes.

INTER.: I am a patient man, performing his job patiently. Isn't it nice just to sit back and look around. Such a clean, bright room. Quite a privilege, isn't it, sight? Not a right, a privilege. We shouldn't take it for granted.

A pause. She screams as he removes her first eye.

SCENE SEVEN

Dorothy and Ezra Pound, on the shore of Tigullio Bay.

DOROTHY: When I first came to Italy I thought that to breathe the same evening air and watch the same sun over the same water would somehow connect me to the ancients; that water, earth and air were constants, one had only to stand in the right place to sense the origin of our values.

EZRA: And now?

DOROTHY: I no longer equate an image with the eternal, no
           matter how beautiful the image, no matter how
           much I wish it would last.

EZRA: It's the aspirations which endure, aspirations allow
           the images to endure.

DOROTHY: Things change. Even hopes change.

EZRA: Once a year, it's a very ancient custom, the local
           women come here, to this bay, to this shore, and
           set lit candles on the water. They put them on trays
           and float the trays out with the tides. It's thought
           to be an ancient fertility rite, first associated with
           Adonis. It's very beautiful to watch, the little lights
           like a thin red necklace on the black water. And
           they sing, the women. In semi-darkness, they sing.

DOROTHY: Songs to Adonis?

EZRA: No, Christian hymns. One tradition swallows
           another.

DOROTHY: Which tradition will swallow the Christian?

EZRA: A matter of some dispute, some anxiety. Whatever
           it is, the roots are already formed. Perhaps we are
           the first tiny blossoms.

DOROTHY: Is that your hope?

EZRA: I admit it. How often do you think I can skip this
           rock?

DOROTHY: I don't know.

EZRA: It's a knack, skipping rocks. In a way it's a picture of
           intelligence.

He throws it.

DOROTHY: Bravo!

EZRA: The mind leaps from reference to reference,
              inference to inference.

DOROTHY: When will we return?

EZRA: Return?

DOROTHY: To England. Simple England.

EZRA: Are you feeling nostalgic about England?
              Simple England?

DOROTHY: Perhaps a little.

EZRA: We left to get away from the hypocrisy.

DOROTHY: I remember.

EZRA: It's probably even worse now.

DOROTHY: At least there was Fleet Street, one got to read the
              different views.

EZRA: There was a certain chaos of strident voices, a
              certain cacophony of daily absurdity captured in
              the headlines, is that what you mean?

DOROTHY: Yes. Exactly.

EZRA: Have you considered the real function of the
              so-called free press: not the intelligent discussion
              of ideas, no, but the creation of public hysteria
              based on meaningless scandal, wiping clean the
              memories of the population day by day. And it
              succeeds admirably. The England I remember is
              a country without a history, the only people who
              thought differently were the tourists.

DOROTHY: You make the confusion sound like a conspiracy.

EZRA:	Not confusion, immorality: the English elite make a financial killing off the money markets, the control of credit, the armament industry. They're parasites. Usury. Medievals called it usura. And the free press? Not a word.
DOROTHY:	You were well respected there.
EZRA:	Was I?
DOROTHY:	Yes.
EZRA:	I was forced to beg for pennies writing reviews of works best forgotten in magazines best ignored.
DOROTHY:	That's not true.
EZRA:	In England, to be well respected isn't to be well employed. In fact, they are held to be mutually exclusive. Here my articles are published in learned journals. I am asked to speak at the Universities. I meet the Head of State. I don't want to return.
DOROTHY:	I want to go home.
EZRA:	When do we admit that the present immorality is not a result of random activity, confusion. It's organized. Organized by certain people and, I could add, certain types of people.
DOROTHY:	Don't you have any doubts, Ezra?
EZRA:	I try to rely upon the facts. Given the right facts, an intelligent interpretation flows easily.
DOROTHY:	It's hard to avoid rhetoric.
EZRA:	It isn't rhetoric.
DOROTHY:	I prefer the silence.
EZRA:	Lethargy?

DOROTHY:	Silence isn't lethargy.
EZRA:	How are we to tell the difference?
DOROTHY:	Why is my silence lethargy and your silence tranquillity?
EZRA:	I didn't say that.
DOROTHY:	You imply it. Ezra, did you leave your son and me a long time ago?
EZRA:	No.
DOROTHY:	Then let's go back, let's go home. Why are we staying? So that you can be closer to Olga?
EZRA:	No.
DOROTHY:	How am I to think otherwise? Have all your friends met her?
EZRA:	It's not important.
DOROTHY:	Ezra, our son …
EZRA:	… is fine.
DOROTHY:	Goes to boarding school in England. Your daughter, your and Olga's daughter, boards with a German speaking family. Your own children have never met. They speak different languages.
EZRA:	I'm aware of that.
DOROTHY:	I am gnawing at the hands of our son. I am on a beach, and every yard apart sits a mother with her child. Olga is there also, and we are all chewing the flesh off our children's hands, like dogs gnawing on bones. The children weep, yet we can only tell that by looking at their faces because we can't hear a sound. When war breaks out I don't want to be here. I want us to be with our child.

EZRA: War used to follow trade paths, now it follows credit lines. If you want to avoid war, then you must change the financial structures.

DOROTHY: Do you need someone to run into your arms? I'll run into your arms. I'll run along the beach into your arms.

EZRA: Are you making fun of me?

DOROTHY: No. I'm trying to remind you …

EZRA: Of what, the things I used to believe? The person I once was?

DOROTHY: Of us. Of our family. Hold me, Ezra. I need you to hold me.

SCENE EIGHT

1939. Benito Mussolini and Claretta Petacci on a luxury traincar to Brenner Pass.

CLARETTA: Why do we enjoy looking at horizons?

BENITO: Because they are far away, and what is close, hurts.

CLARETTA: Hurts?

BENITO: Here, in the head, behind the eyes, it hurts. Is it raining or snowing? Early for snow. Are we almost at the Brenner?

CLARETTA: Gray sky, pale gray mountains.

BENITO: Are we almost there? I need to know. Where are we? How close are we?

CLARETTA: The mountains are the size of delicate ink stains.

BENITO: You have an over-refined temperament, Claretta, anyone would think you had been born rich. If I were to look out the window I wouldn't think of delicate ink stains and … and … whatever.

CLARETTA: Oriental scrolls. No. You think God paints with a trowel. Huge black mountains against a huge white sky.

BENITO: Monumental.

CLARETTA: Very sensitive.

BENITO: Modern. Why do I have to go to meetings when the decisions are already made? There are no decisions. Just ratifications. Ratifications of previous decisions. Whenever I close my eyes I hear barking.

CLARETTA: Most people call it a headache.

BENITO: I have those, too.

CLARETTA: Perhaps it's a conscience. Have you ever considered that?

BENITO: No.

CLARETTA: Why are we persecuting the Jews?

BENITO: Why are you asking?

CLARETTA: You don't often talk about it.

BENITO: It improves our trade relations.

CLARETTA: I don't understand.

BENITO: If you have powerful friends, it's best to walk in step.

CLARETTA: That's all?

BENITO: That's enough. When the English placed a trade embargo on us, who provided us with coal? Germany. The majority of Italians would rather do without Jews than do without coal.

CLARETTA: They weren't asked.

BENITO: You suggest a plebiscite, Jews or coal?

CLARETTA: At least then they'd know the price.

BENITO: We aren't partners with Germany for nothing.

CLARETTA: We were supposed to be partners. They treat us like servants.

BENITO: We have signed an agreement.

CLARETTA: He has only ever lied to us.

BENITO: So? I don't expect the truth, certainly not from Herr Hitler.

CLARETTA: You don't expect the truth from anyone.

BENITO: From you, Claretta, from you.

CLARETTA: Tear up the agreement. Throw the Pact into their faces.

BENITO: Pacts of steel aren't so easily torn.

CLARETTA: Then ignore it. It's only words.

BENITO: It isn't words. No! Not delicate ink stains. Geography! Land! If you can read the map you can read the future. There's a straight line between Berlin and Rome and around this Axis the continent spins.

CLARETTA: The churches are filled with those praying for peace.

BENITO: People are soft.

CLARETTA:	They are holding midnight masses.
BENITO:	They gather in buildings with high ceilings, talk in unison, and believe anything is possible. There is no limit to human stupidity.
CLARETTA:	Your speeches work the same way.
BENITO:	Yes, well, that's not my fault. They always confuse duty with divinity. They've gotten used to it. You fear war, Claretta, you shouldn't. Certain aims are met, certain people die. It's a balance sheet.
CLARETTA:	For the accountants?
BENITO:	Among others.
CLARETTA:	Maybe the Germans are ready for war, but we're not.
BENITO:	Are they better than us?
CLARETTA:	No. Not better. Just stronger.
BENITO:	How is that possible, stronger but not better?
CLARETTA:	We shouldn't fight.
BENITO:	Why not?
CLARETTA:	First, because …
BENITO:	Stop! I don't trust people who count when they answer questions. First, second, third … I don't like that.
CLARETTA:	People like you. They don't like war.
BENITO:	Then they misunderstand me. Strength is defined by its victories. There is only one principle in history. It is to take advantage of the principles of others. You don't think things will stay the way they are? Why

should anyone respect me if all I do is postpone the inevitable? There will be a war. Whether we like it or not Europe will be cut up. I must be at the peace table to stake my claims. I must earn my pair of scissors. True, after I am dead they will dissect my corpse. It is, after all, a political corpse. And they will find a certain rot, a certain, what's the word … intangible smell, traces of blood in the stomach, but that will mean nothing. Dissections don't interest people, power does. I used to pity people, Claretta. I used to pity myself, too, a poor boy with only a labourer's future. That's why I was a socialist. When one has nothing one lives on beliefs, but life is too short for that. Pity is a false belief. It's an evil. It deters one from beginning the difficult climb over the bodies of others. The Socialists believe in pity. They think about purity. They despair because they can't attain perfection. I am successful because I want power. The people understand. In their pig-headed way they understand. Words, my Claretta, words, who is willing to admit the lies they are? I admit it, and that's why the people love me. They trust me because they know I lie. When I speak into a microphone millions listen. Millions beneath the same sky listening to the same voice, is that not inspiring? They don't want to hear the truth, sweet Claretta. The gift they want is the gift of vision. Vision. There is no greater gift that a leader can give.

CLARETTA: Maybe there won't be a war. They didn't fight over Czechoslovakia. They didn't fight over Austria. Why will they fight over Poland? Why go to war over Poland?

SCENE NINE

Dorothy and Ezra at home in Rapallo.

EZRA: Did you listen to my broadcast?

DOROTHY: Yes.

EZRA: You have nothing to say?

DOROTHY: No.

EZRA: Nothing?

DOROTHY: No.

An ellipse of time

EZRA: Did you listen to my broadcast?

DOROTHY: Yes.

EZRA: It was good, wasn't it?

DOROTHY: The income helps.

EZRA: I didn't do it for the income.

DOROTHY: It's the money we're living on.

EZRA: I know that. You have nothing to say?

DOROTHY: No.

An ellipse of time

EZRA: Did you listen to my broadcast?

DOROTHY: Yes.

EZRA: I think they're improving. More pertinent.

DOROTHY: I'm not sure I agree.

EZRA: No?

DOROTHY: No.

An ellipse of time

EZRA: Did you listen to my broadcast?

DOROTHY: Yes.

EZRA: You have nothing to say?

DOROTHY: No.

EZRA: Nothing?

DOROTHY: No.

EZRA: Why are you being so self-effacing?

DOROTHY: Am I?

EZRA: Yes, damn it! Yes!

DOROTHY: I wasn't being self-effacing. I was trying to protect
           a small corner of calm in my mind.

EZRA: I see. Well, by all means, then, let us have quiet.

DOROTHY: What was the mood in Rome?

EZRA: Elated. The continent belongs to the axis.

DOROTHY: Not England.

EZRA: I said the continent, which doesn't include the
           odd island lying to the far Northwest. Besides,
           Churchill will be forced to resign and then
           England will recognize the new world order for
           what it is.

DOROTHY: What is it?

EZRA: A new age, Dorothy.

DOROTHY: From this war …

EZRA: Peace.

DOROTHY: From this butchery?

EZRA: A long peace, resting on new foundations. There
             is a straight line from Berlin to Rome and around
             this axis Europe is reborn. Modern means seeking
             classical ideals.

DOROTHY: I listened to your broadcasts. I wanted very much
             to listen to them. I was very excited, I had so many
             hopes you would … that given the opportunity
             you would say something, something inspired,
             noble, but …

EZRA: You didn't understand.

DOROTHY: If I didn't, who did?

EZRA: I have to assume that there are people who want to
             hear the truth, who are willing to think.

DOROTHY: Yes?

EZRA: And are capable of understanding.

DOROTHY: Ezra, please!

EZRA: I have to assume.

DOROTHY: You talk of so many things at once. You confuse
             issues, you quote from either ridiculous or unknown
             sources. You speak in different accents, slur your
             words, sometimes yell, sometimes whisper.

EZRA: I try to get my points across simply, with emphasis.

DOROTHY: You take all your anger, cut it up into little pieces
             and paste it on the airwaves.

EZRA: Analysis, not anger.

DOROTHY:	Analysis for those who share your prejudices.
EZRA:	I am not prejudiced.
DOROTHY:	The Jews.
EZRA:	The western attitude to money is all wrong.
DOROTHY:	Yes? And?
EZRA:	It's a Jewish attitude.
DOROTHY:	Is it?
EZRA:	And if you hate injustice then you hate that sort of thinking, Jewish thinking, and it's not only Jews who think it.
DOROTHY:	You're sick.
EZRA:	Don't call me sick.
DOROTHY:	Mad.
EZRA:	What?
DOROTHY:	Mad, rabid. You hate Christianity too, why don't you condemn the Christians?
EZRA:	What's good in Christianity derives from the Greeks, what's rotten stems from the Hebrews, you don't have to be a scholar to realize that.
DOROTHY:	Foam on the mouth is not a sign of genius.
EZRA:	They shoot rabid dogs.
DOROTHY:	So others won't become infected.
EZRA:	Why are you always calling me a failure?
DOROTHY:	You speak like one.
EZRA:	When I'm with you I feel like one. You make all my thoughts appear common.

DOROTHY: They're your thoughts.

EZRA: You see what I mean?

DOROTHY: And if your thoughts are common, so what?

EZRA: So what?

DOROTHY: Yes, so what. You have common thoughts,
            common passions, common solutions to common
            problems. They are commonly wrong.

EZRA: I believe in the courage to look at the roots of our
            culture, the very roots, and if they are found to be
            rotten I believe in the courage to pull them.

DOROTHY: To pull them?

EZRA: There is such a thing as human choice. We must
            understand and choose.

DOROTHY: How do you pull these rotten roots? Do we destroy
            everyone who wears different clothing, has a
            different place of worship?

EZRA: I am not talking about destroying people. I am
            talking about clear thinking.

DOROTHY: You are crossing the Acheron and entering hell.

EZRA: Why do you say that?

DOROTHY: You are consenting to evil.

EZRA: I have never hurt anything or anyone in my life.

DOROTHY: Except now, with the only tools you have, words.

EZRA: I should be allowed to say what I think.

DOROTHY: But other persons can't, and they can't because of
            words like yours.

EZRA: After the last war, with all its horrors and futility, after it had ended, and the maimed had returned and the bandages were removed, leaving permanent scars, and we had counted the graves of friends uselessly killed – or have you forgotten them? – and when we asked who was responsible, what was the answer? Noman! Noman built the weapons and Noman bought them. Noman lied about the motivations and Noman conspired in self-interest against the common good. Noman! Noman!

DOROTHY: And now you know his identity. A Jewish banker.

EZRA: The financial institutions built on Jewish attitudes, the usage of credit, the trade wars, the armament industries. God, how much more obvious can it be that these are not random activities?

DOROTHY: You have created a conspiracy and now look for a scapegoat. The Jews are blamed for wrongs for which they are not responsible. You know that Ezra.

EZRA: I am not talking about the corner shopkeeper. I don't care where he prays or how he dresses. I am judging cultural values.

DOROTHY: There are no cultural values without people. You have failed, Ezra. It's a sad sight.

EZRA: Because innocent people get hurt.

DOROTHY: Get killed, yes.

EZRA: What appears as an injustice may in fact be a necessity. It's no use complaining about necessity.

DOROTHY: Necessity. Necessity. Small sibilant stutterings ending in a dying vowel.

EZRA: Necessity is not a trick of the tongue.

DOROTHY:	You have a facility with language that hides the lack of an essential insight. It is frightening.
EZRA:	Why do you hate me?
DOROTHY:	I don't hate you.
EZRA:	You don't understand.
DOROTHY:	I understand your thoughts, Ezra. I understand them as well as anyone, and I forgive them.
EZRA:	I detest you for saying that.
DOROTHY:	Perhaps you are right. Perhaps they shouldn't be forgiven.
EZRA:	This war will be short. It will be short, Dorothy, because the German and Italian societies are healthier than the English. There has been less decay. Less moral rot.

SCENE TEN

Antonio and his brother Pietro. Farm. Southern Italy.

ANTONIO:	How did that thin dried-up old goat of a mother give birth to an ox like you?
PIETRO:	I was smaller at the time.
ANTONIO:	Where's Elena?
PIETRO:	She's out with the child. She'll be back soon.
ANTONIO:	She knew I was coming?
PIETRO:	Yes, yes, we heard. It's been a while Antonio. We haven't seen you for a while.

ANTONIO:	Time passes. Like piss under a bridge. I sent money whenever I could.
PIETRO:	Lately? I haven't seen any money from you for what seems like a long time. What have you been doing?
ANTONIO:	I've been writing for a newspaper.
PIETRO:	They pay?
ANTONIO:	Well …
PIETRO:	What newspaper?
ANTONIO:	A small one. It's time, you know, Elena, I, the boy. I want to come home.
PIETRO:	Good, good.
ANTONIO:	Nothing's wrong? The boy …
PIETRO:	No, no, healthy. My God, he eats and fights, a wonderful boy.
ANTONIO:	The paper I work for, it's a communist paper.
PIETRO:	Communist? You believe in God? You believe in land? You believe in God, you believe in land, and yet you work for the communists.
ANTONIO:	When the army comes down to the south who is in it? The unemployed from the north. And when the army breaks the strikes in the north, who is in it? Peasants from the south who have lost their land.
PIETRO:	So? If you don't have land or a job it's best to join the army. Besides, no-one should be allowed to strike.
ANTONIO:	What do you know about it, asslicker?
PIETRO:	The child, you know, meets other children, plays.
ANTONIO:	Good, that's good.

PIETRO:	Sometimes he calls me papa.
ANTONIO:	You don't tell him that you're his uncle?
PIETRO:	He thinks his uncle … he thinks that his uncle is coming for a visit, today. He thinks his uncle is coming today for a short visit. He's really looking forward to seeing you.
ANTONIO:	Bastard! Bastard!
PIETRO:	Do you want me to break you neck?
ANTONIO:	Where's my wife?
PIETRO:	Later. She'll be here later.
ANTONIO:	You sleep with her? Brother? You sleep with her?
PIETRO:	No.
ANTONIO:	A stupid ox that can't even lie properly.
PIETRO:	Don't call me stupid. She chose.
ANTONIO:	Ignorant peasant.
PIETRO:	It was your idea to go north, not mine. It was you who lost your job, not me. It was you who stopped sending money. I've worked all that time, day in, day out, rain, hot, cold. Years! You want to know where you get arms like this? Working, or have you forgotten? Where were you? Where was the first born? Denying God. Denying the right to own our father's farm. Fighting for the enemy. You are the ignorant peasant.
ANTONIO:	Let me go. Let go of me. What did you and Elena decide?
PIETRO:	We love you like a family loves an uncle, that's all. It's better for everyone.

ANTONIO:	For everyone?
PIETRO:	It's a fact, that's all. Why discuss questions that don't have answers? You can't stay long.

SCENE ELEVEN

Dorothy and Ezra, simple dinner with candles.

DOROTHY:	Before the war friends seemed to find their way, but obviously …
EZRA:	This is civilized.
DOROTHY:	I thought we could pretend we were having guests.
EZRA:	At some point life will return to normal.
DOROTHY:	We have no salt, and the vegetables certainly aren't fresh.
EZRA:	It's not important. A small sacrifice.
DOROTHY:	I know.
EZRA:	America will regret its decision one day. They'll wish they had sided with Berlin and Rome to defeat Moscow. Why is America fighting on the side of Moscow? It's so stupid. Communism is such an aberration of the spirit. You would like to discuss something else.
DOROTHY:	Yes.
EZRA:	Did you listen to the radio?
DOROTHY:	No.
EZRA:	You haven't been listening to the radio?
DOROTHY:	No.

EZRA: Protecting that small corner of your mind?

DOROTHY: Ezra, I want tonight to be special. I am trying to
           make it special.

EZRA: Yes. I suppose.

DOROTHY: You could read aloud later. It's been awhile.

EZRA: I don't know.

DOROTHY: Or I could read aloud. Why not? Cavalcanti's
           sonnets? You're always amused by my Italian
           accent.

EZRA: That's true. Your inability with foreign languages
           has always amazed me.

DOROTHY: I amaze you. That's good.

EZRA: Spoons quietly clinking. Our conversation. I have
           so much to say, to drive into those soft fuzzy heads,
           so many hard facts that need hammering in. When
           I prepare my notes I can't type them fast enough,
           I get frustrated changing paper, changing
           typewriter ribbons.

DOROTHY: It's an anxious time.

EZRA: Goddamn Roosevelt! His ignorance. Why is
           America in this war for Christ's sake? You think it
           has something to do with democracy, I suppose?

DOROTHY: I never said that.

EZRA: You agree with our son who said that. Did anyone
           vote for this war? The last war? Will anyone vote
           for the next war?

DOROTHY: Ezra, our son …

EZRA: … is fine. I'm sure he's fine, tucked into crisp sheets
           in England.

DOROTHY: You don't know, Ezra.

EZRA: There are things we each don't know.

DOROTHY: What are you saying? What are you trying to say?

EZRA: Nothing. What are you trying to say?

DOROTHY: Our son …

EZRA: … is fine. I said so. He's fine. You haven't listened to the BBC.

DOROTHY: No.

EZRA: They read out a list.

DOROTHY: What are you talking about?

EZRA: They read out a list, now that America is in the war, officially in, so to speak, now that America and Italy are officially enemies, someone has been paid to draw up a list.

DOROTHY: Of what?

EZRA: A fairly short list.

DOROTHY: Please, tell me.

EZRA: My broadcasts …

DOROTHY: Yes.

EZRA: I have been indicted for treason by the American government.

DOROTHY: What?

EZRA: My name was on a list. They say my broadcasts aid the enemy, that I am a traitor.

DOROTHY: Your broadcasts are incomprehensible.

EZRA: Clearly not to some. It means if I should ever be
           caught by the Allies then I would be tried.

DOROTHY: For what you say.

EZRA: I have a right, a sacred right to free speech. I am
           invited for my opinions, *my* opinions. No one tells
           me what to say or how to say it.

DOROTHY: No-one need tell you anything. You just happen to
           say all the right things.

EZRA: How could any American jury find me guilty?
           I'm defending the ideals behind the American
           constitution. That's what I'm defending.

DOROTHY: Is it?

EZRA: Yes.

DOROTHY: How?

EZRA: I am willing to take responsibility for my thoughts.
           My conscience, my individual conscience, is guided
           by an understanding of human history. I choose to
           be guided by that understanding. I am Emerson. I
           am Thoreau. I am Whitman.

DOROTHY: I see.

EZRA: Do you?

DOROTHY: No.

EZRA: Why not?

DOROTHY: If you don't choose compassion, then no
           conscience exists at all.

EZRA: No conscience? No conscience?

DOROTHY: No.

EZRA: You know what I think? The Anglo-Saxon race has become so tied down with silly ideas of equality and pity that it has damn well worn down its own genius, its own will to survive.

DOROTHY: Don't talk to me like that. If you want to speak like that on the radio, go ahead! Go ahead! But please don't talk to me like that! I won't stand for it! I won't put up with it!

EZRA: There is a natural hierarchy of ability, in individuals and races. If you block that then everything else goes to hell. That's a fact, not a choice. And it becomes all too apparent in free societies. You hate the logic of my arguments, don't you? It means you have to give up your British hypocrisy, your false sense of pity.

DOROTHY: A natural hierarchy? Of ability? And should we be bred like cattle? The best heifer? The best bull?

EZRA: Courtship is a slow form of eugenics, choosing the appropriate mate. But there must be better means. Less romantic. More scientific.

DOROTHY: I hate you! I hate you, Ezra. I spit! I spit at you! Our son is not an example of a race. He's a boy, just a boy. Our son is a boy we conceived in gentleness, who was born with joy. And he has written to us. He has written …

EZRA: What did he say?

DOROTHY: He has joined the American army. He expects to be sent to the European front.

EZRA: Why did he do a damn-fool thing like that? Why is he risking his life for the kike money merchants of London? Why is he such a fool?

DOROTHY:	Read the letter. It's quite … eloquent.
EZRA:	Give it to me. Good. I'm going to burn it. I'm going to burn this damn thing. I don't ever want to see it.

He burns the letter.

EZRA:	Good. Good.
DOROTHY:	This is civilized, isn't it? Is that what you said earlier? Civilized? Tell me, is there any sight more horrifying than this civilization? Ezra, help me, I want to throw up. Oh Jesus, Ezra, I can't take it anymore.
EZRA:	Dorothy, I'm sorry. Here's something. I'll wipe it up.
DOROTHY:	I can't take it. I can't. There's no peace anywhere, not in the world, not in my mind. Oh god. It hurts. My whole body hurts. I'm not myself, I can't control …
EZRA:	I know. I know.
DOROTHY:	Apologize, Ezra, apologize.
EZRA:	No.
DOROTHY:	Admit that you're frightened. Admit that it comes from your fear.
EZRA:	No.
DOROTHY:	Admit it. Say it. Tell me.
EZRA:	I can't deny what I believe.
DOROTHY:	Tell me!
EZRA:	No!
DOROTHY:	Say it!
EZRA:	No!
DOROTHY:	Tell me! "I apologize. I am afraid."

EZRA:	No.
DOROTHY:	You are a religious man with a political God. It must be frightening.
EZRA:	I must go back to Rome soon.
DOROTHY:	How will you ever explain to our son?
EZRA:	I won't be convicted. Free speech is guaranteed in the constitution.
DOROTHY:	You've made ashes of his words.
EZRA:	I'll stay the night and return to Rome tomorrow.
DOROTHY:	Ashes. I once loved you, but now I find even that idea morally reprehensible.

SCENE TWELVE

Clear night. Pietro is calling Antonio in an empty field.

| PIETRO: | Antonio! Antonio! Antonio! |

Antonio emerges

ANTONIO:	Why did you find me?
PIETRO:	Antonio.
ANTONIO:	Why?
PIETRO:	I'm your brother.
ANTONIO:	That's a reason?
PIETRO:	Lot of stars.
ANTONIO:	Each one is a bullet hole.
PIETRO:	Lot of bullet holes.

ANTONIO:	How's my son?
PIETRO:	Your son is hungry. He's fine. I want to fight.
ANTONIO:	You do?
PIETRO:	Yes.
ANTONIO:	On whose side?
PIETRO:	Beside you.
ANTONIO:	You don't believe what I believe.
PIETRO:	So what? We share an enemy.
ANTONIO:	How did you find that out?
PIETRO:	Nothing has been easy.
ANTONIO:	No.
PIETRO:	Nothing.
ANTONIO:	Nothing.
ANTONIO:	How's Elena?
PIETRO:	I have to piss.
ANTONIO:	So go piss. You can do that by yourself.
PIETRO:	There's a dead body over here.
ANTONIO:	There are dead bodies everywhere. Piss in the other direction. Against the wind. Piss against the wind.
PIETRO:	It's a young woman.
ANTONIO:	Death has no age! No sex! Idiot! Let him look at it. Hold it. Caress it. Let him love the dead. He's a Catholic. It's allowed. Think: he goes to the priest and says: "Father, I have sinned." So the priest asks: "How did you sin my son?" And he says: "I had relations with a woman, Father." So the

priest asks: "And did you have to pay, my son?"
And he answers: "No, I didn't have to pay." So the
priest considers and says: "Well, my son, in these
troubled times to love a woman is not so great a
sin, perhaps you can ask her to marry." And my
brother says: "I asked, Father, I whispered in her
ear, marry me, marry me, but she didn't answer."
The priest now comes to his conclusion: "Well,
my son, I see that your intentions were good, and
I have known many cases where woman have led
men into temptation. Clearly, the fault is not yours.
Go in peace." What took you so long?

PIETRO: There was that dead body. I covered it with
newspapers and some stones. It's sad. So many
dead bodies. Antonio, I am sad so often. Antonio,
this is the happiest I have been in a long time,
looking up at the stars with you.

ANTONIO: How's Elena?

PIETRO: She died, Antonio. There was a riot for food. The
police shot on us. The boy is with his aunt.

ANTONIO: She died.

PIETRO: Full of bullet holes. From our own police. The
women were at the front, beating their pots,
chanting for food, for fair prices. I saw her shot. I
saw her shot so many times. I held her. Antonio,
I held her. I swear to God I will kill them. I don't
need a gun, Antonio. Just let me get at them. Let
me get close, I swear, I swear to you, Antonio.
I held her and she was bleeding from so many
places. I was trying to clean her face. I was licking
her face. Let me help you, Antonio. There is
nothing else I want to do. We buried her, your boy
and I. You'd like him, Antonio. He works hard.

SCENE THIRTEEN

Benito Mussolini and Claretta Petacci. Salo, 1943.

BENITO: Government is a technique of domination, I had forgotten, but I remember now. Perhaps it is not too late.

CLARETTA: Too late for what?

BENITO: How can you ask?

CLARETTA: For honour?

BENITO: That word.

CLARETTA: We are all living on borrowed time.

BENITO: What do you suggest?

CLARETTA: As a final gesture?

BENITO: To get control.

CLARETTA: There is nothing to be done.

BENITO: Nothing?

CLARETTA: You have been overthrown. It's simple.

BENITO: I was betrayed.

CLARETTA: Overthrown by your own government. Imprisoned by party hacks of your own choosing.

BENITO: I am free. I have been set free.

CLARETTA: By the Germans.

BENITO: With German assistance.

CLARETTA: Holed up in a resort hotel smelling of sauerkraut, head of a republic that doesn't exist.

BENITO: It is a disagreeable trait, isn't it, their love of rancid food?

CLARETTA: Colonel Dolmann has suggested the disarming of all Italian troops.

BENITO: Colonel Dolmann is ridiculous.

CLARETTA: Why? Our soldiers defect to the partisans and take their weapons with them. Why should the Germans supply both sides of a civil war?

BENITO: You talk nonsense. You talk like a person condemned.

CLARETTA: Why are we being kept alive?

BENITO: I am an inspiration to the men who fight.

CLARETTA: You are useful for propaganda. Your name is useful for propaganda. And when a defector is captured he's tortured. I don't know why. They only tell us what we already know. Did you know I watch the torture? I expect to learn something.

BENITO: I don't watch it. It's disgusting.

CLARETTA: You order it.

BENITO: Not for my amusement.

CLARETTA: A technique.

BENITO: Justice must be felt to be done. Responsibilities aren't pleasant. I am fulfilling responsibilities.

CLARETTA: I used to turn my eyes but now I watch it all. I watch with the same feeling as at my first communion, when I knew something incomprehensible and vaguely sick and ridiculous was happening, but everyone was pleased to see it. Drink the blood. Eat the flesh. Redemption. That's what I'm looking

for when I watch, that moment of redemption,
and in the filth and pain that moment of grace,
divine mercy. But it never comes. Not in front of
me and not in my mind. I never see it. You say I am
condemned. By who? By who am I condemned?

BENITO: I will defeat this anti-Fascist reaction. I can defeat
it. Given a choice between communism and
ourselves the people will always choose us.

CLARETTA: That's not the choice any more.

BENITO: I will tell them what the choice is. I will tell them
what to think.

CLARETTA: In peace time they might listen. In a war they know
they're losing they make up their own minds.

BENITO: I tell you they will listen. They will see their
choices, no, their one choice, and then they will
flock to me. They will raise me with their voices,
shouting in unison, ecstatic: "Viva! Viva!" We
will sing the old songs. Bonfires will burn on the
beaches. Everyone will dance with the flames. We
will shoot those who sulk in the shadows. It is
time to be hard, to stand erect. I will be hard. I will
fondle the people until they are hard. You are not
laughing. You must learn to laugh. We laugh so as
not to be frightened. Claretta, my love, my mother
my child, come here. That's it. Closer.

CLARETTA: Do you have a camera, Benito? Do you know
how to take pictures? I would like you to take my
picture. I will stand here and smile, a slight smile
because I don't want anyone to see my teeth. I
hate my mouth. That's why I never smile. You say
that it's very important to laugh. Laugh so as not
to go crazy, but my teeth are rotting behind my
lips. How can I laugh? How can I smile? Take my

picture and make me look like I did when I first
met you, when I was young and beautiful and
almost a woman. And sign the back of it, and date
it, and add some silly words. You must ratify it. But
choose another name, Benito, another name, or I'll
have to rip the picture up. I'll rip it anyway. There,
I've ripped it. It falls like confetti on my shoes. I
am very happy now, here with you. Do you know
why I am happy? Because the end is in sight. Oh,
God! I want to die! I want everything to die! I want
everything, everything, everything to die.

BENITO: You are beautiful. So beautiful.

CLARETTA: Not like this, Benito. Let's lie down. I will hold you
softly. I will hold you close.

BENITO: No, I don't want that. I want your mouth. I want
your mouth. You hate that, don't you? But you do
it. That's what I want to see. Your self-hatred. Your
self-hatred keeps me alive. Ah! Ah!!

CLARETTA: You always whimper when you come. You come
like a little boy sniffling with a cold.

SCENE FOURTEEN

Grazia cooking at a small fire, beside railway tracks. Enter Ezra.

EZRA: Who are you?

GRAZIA: Why do you want to know?

EZRA: You are cooking something. I'm hungry.

GRAZIA: You want to steal it.

EZRA: I've been walking for two days without food.
Two days.

GRAZIA:	That's not long.
EZRA:	I'm following the tracks. Two days. I'm hoping that a train will pass.
GRAZIA:	Will you get on it?
EZRA:	If it goes north. I'm trying to get home.
GRAZIA:	Why?
EZRA:	The government has deserted Rome. The city is in chaos. The city has fallen.
GRAZIA:	Is a city fallen when the rats have fled?
EZRA:	It's the government which has fled.
GRAZIA:	Then the city is liberated.
EZRA:	It's a cold night. Clear and cold.
GRAZIA:	Is anything clear?
EZRA:	Blind?
GRAZIA:	A blind beggar.
EZRA:	It smells good.
GRAZIA:	Why should I share it? I don't know you.
EZRA:	I'm hungry.
GRAZIA:	No.
EZRA:	I need something to eat.
GRAZIA:	Eat.
EZRA:	It's good.
GRAZIA:	I was sitting still and humming. It came up to me whining. It wanted a little petting, a little warmth. I broke its neck.

EZRA:	What is it?
GRAZIA:	I eat with my fingers, only my fingers. I don't need … spoons. Soup I drink from the bowl. I don't have any soup.
EZRA:	What is it?
GRAZIA:	No more questions. Please. No more. I won't answer. No names. I won't give names.
EZRA:	What names?
GRAZIA:	I hear a train. Listen.
EZRA:	I hear nothing.
GRAZIA:	But as you say, there are tracks. Perhaps a train. It's coming this way. I can hear it. Will you get on it? Let's sing. We can sing rounds. I start then you join in, or you can start, I'll join in. Sing. Sing.
EZRA:	What are you hearing?
GRAZIA:	No more questions. Please. No more. I won't answer. I don't know any names. I don't know any names. Leave a little light, please, a little light.
EZRA:	You're mad. You must be mad.
GRAZIA:	Yes, mad. Mad. Insane. Concentrate. Concentrate. The wind is singing. The wind and the children are holding hands and singing, among the ashes.
EZRA:	A train.
GRAZIA:	The labour camp trains. The concentration camp trains. The death trains. A system designed, a few orders give and then nothing is left. I see nothing.
EZRA:	Apparitions.
GRAZIA:	Trains. Concentrate. Car after car. Car after car.

	Supply and demand. Supply and demand. We can sing rounds. You begin and I join in.
EZRA:	Car after car. Car after car.
GRAZIA:	Cheap labour needed, poor bodies supplied. Supply and demand. Supply and demand. A system designed, a few orders given, and then nothing remains.
EZRA:	Apparitions.
GRAZIA:	Faces, faces on death trains.
EZRA:	Car after car, car, car.
GRAZIA:	No more questions. Please. No more. I won't answer. I don't know any names. I don't know any names. Leave a little light, please, a little light. The wind and the children are holding hands and singing, among the ashes. The labour camp trains. The concentration camp trains. The death trains. A system designed, a few orders given and then nothing is left. I see nothing.
EZRA:	Caw! Caw! Caw.

SCENE FIFTEEN

*Overlapping conversations. Ezra and Dorothy in one,
Benito, Claretta, Antonio and Pietro in another.*

EZRA:	I'm afraid, Dorothy.
PIETRO:	What do we do?
ANTONIO:	We let him go for a walk in the woods. The whore can guide him.
PIETRO:	He's quiet.

ANTONIO: An unexpected improvement.

DOROTHY: The American Army has landed on the coast.
             It's better to hand yourself over to them than to
             be caught by the Partisans. They would kill you
             without a trial.

EZRA: I know.

CLARETTA: You are going to shoot him.

ANTONIO: Yes.

CLARETTA: Why?

ANTONIO: Shooting him is ripping a poster off a wall. There is
             no difference.

EZRA: I want a trial. I have always believed that to
             understand something is to call it by its right
             name. Let them decide my name.

CLARETTA: You'll shoot him without a trial?

ANTONIO: The trial is over.

CLARETTA: A simple question. To the other one. You are Italian?

PIETRO: From the South.

CLARETTA: Do you feel nothing for him?

PIETRO: A desire to see him dead, and once dead, to see
             him killed again.

CLARETTA: I will walk. We will walk. Have faith, Benito. I have
             faith. Let's go towards the trees. The shade. Yes.

They walk, Claretta turns.

CLARETTA: No, this is wrong, You can't! You can't!

Claretta is shot, Mussolini turns, is shot.

EZRA: Are you all right?

DOROTHY: I'm fine.

ANTONIO: You all right?

PIETRO: I'm fine. Calm.

DOROTHY: You look pale.

EZRA: I feel pale.

ANTONIO: Put the bodies in the truck. We're going to Milan.

*Mussolini and Claretta are strung upside down by Pietro
and Antonio.*

PIETRO: We'll hang them upside down as they will hang
           in hell. We'll let the wind, the rain, the birds clean
           their flesh until nothing remains except the bones,
           and the sins which are the marrow of those bones.

ANTONIO: You're talking like a Catholic. If we string them up
           it will be to show that authority can be overthrown,
           that's all. No-one is so large or powerful he can't be
           cut down and strung up.

SCENE SIXTEEN

*1945. Washington, DC, USA, Dr. Overholser, psychiatrist,
and Ezra Pound are in a consulting room of St. Elizabeth's Hospital
for the Criminally Insane.*

EZRA: Why should I talk to you?

DOCTOR: You don't have to.

EZRA: But you are … you want to listen to what I say.

DOCTOR: It is my job.

EZRA: Being a psychiatrist. And you, what brings you to the nation's capital, the cerebellum of the United States of America, the five-star ganglia of the New World? I know why I'm here.

DOCTOR: My name is Dr. Overholser. I am the director of the hospital. I've been asked to assist in evaluating your mental condition.

EZRA: Before the trial?

DOCTOR: Yes.

EZRA: Before the kangaroos gather. Bad image. Wrong continent. Before the jackasses bray. The human mind is difficult to understand.

DOCTOR: We are fortunate to have such excellent tools.

EZRA: Words.

DOCTOR: Yes.

EZRA: So I have to be careful.

DOCTOR: On the contrary. Speak as you usually would.

EZRA: I want to defend myself at the trial. In court I would like to be my own counsel.

DOCTOR: The crime is considered too serious. You must have legal counsel. That is the law.

EZRA: The law must be interpreted.

DOCTOR: I believe that is why counsel is obligatory.

EZRA: I am my own judge. I understand the issues and I am my own judge.

DOCTOR: What happened after you handed yourself in?

EZRA: You know I turned myself in?

DOCTOR: Yes.

EZRA: I was an America citizen turning myself over to American soldiers on Italian soil. I expected protection.

DOCTOR: And?

EZRA: They imprisoned me.

DOCTOR: You didn't know you had been indicted for treason?

EZRA: I was put in a cage … a cage.

DOCTOR: Didn't you hand yourself in because you knew you had been indicted for treason by the American Government? Didn't you know you had been charged?

EZRA: Yes. I knew.

DOCTOR: Perhaps you were also frightened by the anti-Fascist reaction at the end of the war. Perhaps you were frightened for your own personal safety.

EZRA: No. I wasn't frightened. Not for my safety.

DOCTOR: It would have been normal.

EZRA: And that's what you seek, isn't it? The normal, the mundane, the mediocre.

DOCTOR: And after you handed yourself in?

EZRA: I was put in a cage. It was called the Pisan Detention center, but it was just a few rows of cages, cages without roofs. There were a few buildings for the guards, a medical dispensary. There was a typewriter in the dispensary.

DOCTOR: You used the typewriter.

EZRA: Yes. Not at the beginning, but eventually.

DOCTOR:	What did you write about?
EZRA:	I'm not sure. Purgatory, the beginnings of paradise.
DOCTOR:	A literary vision?
EZRA:	My … interpretation. My … fragments.
DOCTOR:	You wrote in the cage?
EZRA:	Mostly, and then transcribed my notes in the dispensary. Next to me, in another cage, was a black man from South Carolina. Such a beautiful face, a perfect African mask. He called me "little white mouse".
DOCTOR:	Why did he call you "little white mouse"?
EZRA:	He said I squeaked in my sleep, and that I always slept huddled in a corner.
DOCTOR:	Did you mind him calling you that?
EZRA:	No. When it rained we had no shelter. Nothing but sky over our heads. Once I mentioned the smell of mint growing outside the cage. After it rains you can smell the mint. That's what gave him the idea I was killing spiders. If you kill spiders, he said, then it rains, if it rains, you smell the mint.
DOCTOR:	Were you killing spiders?
EZRA:	I don't know. It's hardly important. I suppose I killed a few. Boredom. I don't know. I didn't mutilate them. I didn't pull off their legs one by one, I just … in any case it doesn't cause rain.
DOCTOR:	Can you describe the smell of that mint?
EZRA:	It's the smell of relief. The scent of starting over.
DOCTOR:	Do you want to start over?

EZRA:	The black man from Carolina didn't. He said he was hoping to be convicted, killed and cremated all on the same day. I remember that clearly.
DOCTOR:	It meant something to you when he said that.
EZRA:	He said he didn't want to be buried because he'd been buried all his life, and he liked cremations because they hardly left any traces. I've spent so much time creating traces.
DOCTOR:	The writing?
EZRA:	Yes.
DOCTOR:	Why was he being held in the detention center?
EZRA:	Insubordination. I suppose you could call it that. He aimed a flame thrower at an officer who had called him a dirty lousy nigger.
DOCTOR:	How long were you in the cage?
EZRA:	Six months. I'm told.
DOCTOR:	The reports indicate a sudden change in behaviour during your stay.
EZRA:	I was afraid. I acted afraid. Sometimes.
DOCTOR:	It's normal to be afraid while awaiting trial for treason. Is that what you meant when you said you were afraid?
EZRA:	No.
DOCTOR:	You meant something else?
EZRA:	I was afraid of everything. Not just the future. I was afraid of the past.
DOCTOR:	Can you continue that thought?
EZRA:	No. Have you talked to Dorothy?

DOCTOR:	Briefly.
EZRA:	I want you to tell her something.
DOCTOR:	You can tell her yourself.
EZRA:	She hates me. You must know that.
DOCTOR:	I don't think she hates you.
EZRA:	Sometimes I liked the cage. It protected me.
DOCTOR:	From?
EZRA:	Others. I want you to tell her I'm sorry.
DOCTOR:	You can tell her yourself.
EZRA:	No.
DOCTOR:	What are you sorry for?
EZRA:	I don't know. I'm not sure.
DOCTOR:	Why can't you talk to her?
EZRA:	I try to talk … to her … no words. Tired. Tired. I want to yell.
DOCTOR:	You want to yell at Dorothy?
EZRA:	Yes.
DOCTOR:	Why?
EZRA:	To scream and yell. Because I hurt her. She's telling me I hurt her. She's telling me.
DOCTOR:	Has she told you that?
EZRA:	She talking to me now. I can hear her now, telling me.
DOCTOR:	There's no-one here but us.
EZRA:	They're here.
DOCTOR:	What are they saying?

EZRA: I don't know.

DOCTOR: I hear only silence Mr. Pound.

EZRA: Would you close the window, Dorothy! The sounds
           are bothering me. I'm trying to think.

DOCTOR: Mr. Pound ...

EZRA: Close the window, for Christ's sake! Stop that
           noise! Stop that!

DOCTOR: I know that you can hear me. I know that
           you understand.

EZRA: *Caw! Caw!!* I know exactly what I'm doing.
           I always have. Tell Dorothy that.

DOCTOR: Why are you pretending to hear voices? Why are
           you pretending to be a crow?

EZRA: The sky above the cages was often quite beautiful.

DOCTOR: Are you hoping to be found mentally unfit
           to stand trial?

EZRA: Rain clouds above, dust below, legless spiders in
           the dust.

DOCTOR: If you stand trial you may be convicted. The
           sentence for treason can be death. If you are found
           mentally unfit for trial you won't suffer that sentence
           but you won't be released either. You will be held,
           here, at St. Elizabeth's Hospital, with other mentally
           ill patients. You will be held indefinitely. I repeat my
           question. Why are you pretending to be a crow?

EZRA: I want to write paradise, having been to hell. Do
           you think I'm closer to achieving that as a bird
           than as a man? I dreamt about the black man, I
           wanted him in the cell with me, with his little white
           mouse. On sunny days, in the heat, I wanted ... In

	court I would like to defend myself. Who decides if I'm mentally unfit?
DOCTOR:	Three psychiatrists. Myself and two others. We will talk to you and observe you over a period of time.
EZRA:	I defended the American constitution in a foreign country. That's all I did. Did anyone tell you that? That during the war I defended the constitution? That, apparently, is my shame.
DOCTOR:	My understanding is that you are accused of accepting employment with the Italian government as a radio propagandist. My understanding is that you incited racial hatred and demoralization among the troops.
EZRA:	I am not a Fascist!
DOCTOR:	You are not being accused of being a Fascist.
EZRA:	What is a Fascist? Do you know? Any idea? You think we're all sick, don't you? You want to treat it like an illness, some … problem of the mind.
DOCTOR:	Is that what you want me to think?
EZRA:	It's all right to act like a Fascist in America as long as you talk like a Christian.
DOCTOR:	Why do you say that?
EZRA:	We were millions. Millions. Do you think that each of us, individually, was sick?
DOCTOR:	You began to speak of certain erotic dreams, would you like to continue?
EZRA:	You don't know how to deal with it, do you? There's a world war and you think it's caused by mental illness, or repressed sexual desires. You're not willing to look at the facts, are you?

DOCTOR:	Do you have difficulty maintaining feelings of self-respect while with members of the opposite sex?
EZRA:	I don't understand the question.
DOCTOR:	No?
EZRA:	I understand the words, but not the question.
DOCTOR:	The words?
EZRA:	I don't understand your intentions, so I can't understand your questions. I am talking calmly, aren't I?
DOCTOR:	Yes.
EZRA:	But I want to kill you. I want to cut off your head.
DOCTOR:	What causes this rage in you?
EZRA:	I don't know. I'm not angry. I'm dead. A drowned dog …
DOCTOR:	That caws.
EZRA:	Caws?
DOCTOR:	Earlier you were cawing like a crow.
EZRA:	Was I?
DOCTOR:	I have noticed, over and over, that when we believe that nothing can change we talk of human nature in animal terms or racist terms, something bestial, something fixed.
EZRA:	I have always had faith in change.
DOCTOR:	A drowned dog cawing is hardly a symbol of change.
EZRA:	My words are precise. I have studied ancient cultures, learned ancient languages, seeking that precision. I have studied the most enduring masks.

DOCTOR: Masks?

EZRA: Yes.

DOCTOR: They help you?

EZRA: To juggle. I juggle masks. I juggle personae. How often do you think I can skip a rock?

DOCTOR: I would like to talk about your rage.

EZRA: We don't speak the same language. After my breakdown they gave me a tent, a tent in a cage, a triangle in a square. They gave me medication, too. I was having trouble urinating, the pain. I needed the medication.

DOCTOR: I have your medical reports.

EZRA: Would you like to know when I found out about the concentration camps? It was after Rome had fallen.

DOCTOR: But before that, you were there, did you think it was all in the abstract?

EZRA: At the end of the war I saw pictures in an issue of *Time* magazine. There were atrocities on both sides. Do you think it's propaganda, the pictures?

DOCTOR: No.

EZRA: How do you know?

DOCTOR: Are you surprised by the horror of which we are systematically capable?

EZRA: Are you?

DOCTOR: No.

EZRA: Having studied the human mind?

DOCTOR: Having studied the human condition.

EZRA: Which can be changed?

DOCTOR: It begins with speech. Talking.

EZRA: Speech is memory. Judgment.

DOCTOR: Without the possibility of change speech is a mask for silence.

EZRA: Dr. Overholser, you are German. You have a German name.

DOCTOR: Does that lessen me in your eyes?

EZRA: On the contrary.

DOCTOR: I wish you hadn't said that. I will present my views to the court. The prosecution has a chance to cross-examine my findings, and then there will be a judgment. However, if all three examining psychiatrists concur then it is difficult for the judge to go against their testimony.

EZRA: And will they concur? That I am …

DOCTOR: Mentally unfit? I don't know.

EZRA: Holding me indefinitely in an insane asylum is still imprisonment. Am I not innocent until proven guilty, or is it different for the mentally unfit?

DOCTOR: You seem to have a good grasp of the situation.

EZRA: I want a trial. I want to defend myself.

DOCTOR: To use the trial as a platform?

EZRA: The psychiatrist is a dog catcher. He silences rabid animals before they wake the sleeping. You muzzle us with dream analysis.

DOCTOR:	Do I?
EZRA:	Clearly.
DOCTOR:	What are the moral benefits of your state execution?
EZRA:	You are suggesting that I should be thankful for being held here indefinitely?
DOCTOR:	Frankly?
EZRA:	You think I'm guilty.
DOCTOR:	That's up to the jury.
EZRA:	What do you think?
DOCTOR:	Feelings of patriotism run strong after a war. That is understandable. I should know, my lineage is, as you point out, German. That is all I will say. While you are here I will do everything I can to make you as comfortable as possible, as I would any patient. You have said you wanted time to write your paradise, perhaps you will, perhaps you won't, but here you will have quiet and time. The grounds at St. Elizabeth's are quite good. There are trees with squirrels. Guests are permitted, not at first, but later. One can lunch on the grass. Some of the patients are quite entertaining.
EZRA:	Quite. Entertaining.
DOCTOR:	Given recent history, this insane asylum, your words, is a perfect city of the mind. It has a certain order. It's not particularly vicious. One escapes the past.

SCENE SEVENTEEN

We are on the grounds of the insane asylum. Ezra sits at a distance, talking to himself. Autumn leaves are spread over the playing area. There is a small foot bridge. Dorothy enters and approaches a young man raking the leaves.

EZRA: I return to an empty room and am met by an image of you in an empty room; you are reading. You feel the relief upon those bruised pages, our son. Your head turns towards me. I watch beads of sweat in creases of your neck like streams caught among pebbles. I am a crow, Dorothy, see me hidden among the twisting limbs, perched on a hollow branch, cawing, a crow, Dorothy, a crumpled shadow in the shallow waters of a receding tide. My beak open, my wings broken, I've drowned in repeating patterns I cannot understand.

DOROTHY: Excuse me, I am looking for someone.

The young man shakes his head.

Y. MAN: English, no good.

DOROTHY: *Lei parla italiano?*

Y. MAN: *Si, signora. Sono italiano.*

DOROTHY: *Nato in Italia?*

Y. MAN: *Si, sono arrivato solo da poco. I miei genitori sono morti durante la guerra. Ma ho uno zio, un uomo buono assai, e stato lui a farmi venire in America. Que posso ricominciare da capo in un paese nuovo. Sono molto grato agli americani. Ho perfino gia trovato un lavoro, come giardiniere. Domani chi sa?*

DOROTHY: *Mio marito e uno dei pazienti. M'hanno detto di cercarlo in giardino, ma non mi riesce di trovarlo.*

EZRA: I knew a woman, I knew a woman. A goddess standing against the evening light. So beautiful. A spirit floating in the azure air. What was her name, the woman I once knew?

DOROTHY: *Grazie. Ce bel cielo!*

Y. MAN: Yes. Beautiful.

EZRA: Why can't I remember her name? Small fragments of remembering that, to be coherent, call, call forth, calling.

DOROTHY: Ezra?

EZRA: Do I have to go in soon? I can't tell if it's dawn or dusk.

DOROTHY: Ezra.

EZRA: The man you are looking for isn't here. Keep going. There are cardboard men everywhere. They wander about. Perhaps he's one of them.

DOROTHY: I'm looking for the one who walked with me in Kensington Gardens, who recited the Poets of Provence and knew the sonnets of Cavalcanti.

EZRA: I have heard of him, but I have never looked him in the face.

DOROTHY: Am I disturbing you?

EZRA: Do you know what paradise is, Dorothy? It is small fragments, shards of memory. It is a discontinuous jangling, like loose change clinking in a pocket.

DOROTHY: Your poems are being read again.

EZRA: Nothing like a little press, a little controversy.

DOROTHY: You have always wanted to stir your readers into action, but it's your words of resignation that stir them the most. They find your cries of despair and humility, what they take to be despair and humility, quite ... They find it beautiful.

EZRA: It's not what I intended. I despise them for thinking my despair romantic or beautiful.

DOROTHY: What were your intentions?

EZRA: When I am silent I hear other voices. It has always been so.

DOROTHY: I don't accept that.

EZRA: Small fragments of remembering that, to be coherent, call, call forth, calling. They contradict. Now what? One thought. Another. Let the contradictions speak. I scratch in the dust, words? The wind stirs the dust, singing? Small fragments that, to be coherent ...

DOROTHY: Ezra, talk to me. Don't polish the fragments. Talk. It is quite pleasant tonight. Pleasant. Not quite Rapallo. not quite the Bay of Tigullio. I have started water colours again. Nothing major. Just pictures of my potted plants on the window sill. I have been walking around the city. There is a great deal of white marble, huge buildings with wise sayings cut into them, spacious roads, a tangible order to everything. This is the city of your dreams, Ezra. I always thought that Washington would be like London, but it's not. It's much more like Rome. So Imperial.

EZRA: Have you found an apartment?

DOROTHY: A small basement apartment, but clean. It's not far from her, close to Capitol Hill. Sometimes in the evening I find myself humming. I quite like living alone.

EZRA: Have you heard from our son?

DOROTHY: Yes. He says he will visit soon. He says he looks forward to meeting you.

EZRA: What is that scratching sound?

DOROTHY: The gardener is raking leaves. He's just a young man from Italy, a recent immigrant.

EZRA: You talked to him?

DOROTHY: Yes, I find it easier now, to talk to people. He has no family left in Italy, they died in the war, all except for one uncle who arranged for him to come here. He overflows with gratitude at finding himself in America.

EZRA: A gardener in an insane asylum. Dorothy, I want to hold you.

DOROTHY: No, I don't want to lie any more.

EZRA: What lie?

DOROTHY: To myself. There are no cycles. We can't begin again.

EZRA: Memories are a cage, a cage.

DOROTHY: They needn't be.

EZRA: They are.

DOROTHY: The judge has found with the psychiatrists. You won't be tried. You will have time.

EZRA: On grounds of insanity?

DOROTHY: You were found mentally unfit to stand trial.

EZRA: Will I ever be released?

DOROTHY:	There can always be an executive pardon. The lawyer seems to feel that when the issues die down, and the facts are forgotten, when you've become a stray piece of paper on a bureaucrat's desk, then, perhaps, a pardon might be arranged, on the grounds of pity.
EZRA:	Of pity. Freed on the grounds of pity, when I am an old and toothless man, when I am forgotten.
DOROTHY:	Yes.
EZRA:	Oblivion will be my release.
DOROTHY:	It is for us all.
EZRA:	You say that very calmly.
DOROTHY:	I am calm. I have faith.
EZRA:	In what?
DOROTHY:	Oh, I don't know. Perhaps in the fact that this insane asylum has a gardener.
EZRA:	You place your faith in small things.
DOROTHY:	Yes and no.
EZRA:	The will of one person?
DOROTHY:	No.
EZRA:	The will of many?
DOROTHY:	No.
EZRA:	What then?
DOROTHY:	The compassion native to us all.
EZRA:	To us all?

DOROTHY: Yes.

EZRA: Is it enough? Is it strong enough? When you walk
             though the city beyond the wall of this garden of
             ghosts, tell me, is your compassion enough?

THE CONSOLATION
OF PHILOSOPHY

———

BOOK ONE

An impoverished Boethius writes ten sonnets on the subject of geese.

–1–

Douloureux, triste, mur sale.
Byzantium fallen here
on Fort Street, solid state
pictograms, the scent of
pissed concrete; home, yes,
beneath schematic fucks
and random numbers, a place
to lay one's head for those
who dream of geese.

The siege continues: greed,
false ownership, shameless
lies and purchased virtue.
The stresses are financial:
the fossil is aesthetic.

2

Geese fly on this grey wall.
They, above the rivers
of piss, own nothing, bank
with averted gaze, soar
with intimated limbs
on cracked foundations
of concrete. Here, tonight,
I will sleep. Tomorrow
I will eat, if I can.

To you I am monstrous.
Ugly, dirty, I touch
myself and sing out loud.
I bang my bleeding head.
Geese, geese, drawn in red

The shadow of the goose
has disappeared; not seen,
though fossils are seen, washed
clean on small beachstones
smooth to the inquiring
touch. Fossils, seen
and smooth, turned beneath
lapping waves, turning
and sucked on the wet tongue.

God, such pretentiousness,
these sly words. Both hands
so I fashion shadows:—
a silly goose lives, flies,
swallows silence,

Pomme de reinette et pomme
d'api, petit tapis
rouge, pomme de reinette
et pomme d'api, petit
tapis gris:—so singeth
the children, falling
into leaves, autumnal
dissonances of youth and age,
a gathering of waxed colours.

There's a bite in the air.
Shadows are hard. Certain
streams are frozen. People say
"Collect!" I have nothing
to gather. Emigrate?

flecks of champagne on seas
of sorrow, that is America.
Born in the U.S.A., thirsting
after flecks, foaming beer,
glass underfoot, postcards
of geese on the wall. The Man
with the Crotch, The Woman with
the Crotch, rise from the Marsh,
champagne glasses break
across their faces. Applause.

I am from the North. I am
from the North. I am from the
North. I am from the North.
I am from the North.

6

You eat and talk, eat and
talk psychology. Bah!
You are crude. Fear
moves you. Greed moves you. Both
move you in the same direction:—
a known statistic
you plead isolation.
You are smooth like a graph.
Over good wine, cooked goose,
you confess loneliness.

It sticks in my throat. Tell,
you who stutter, stutter,
where comes this fallacy?
Matters of policy?

Geese fly on this grey wall.
Red geese on this grey wall.
Drawn red intimations
of geese on this wall. Grey
sky streaked with thought. Flecks
of red on this grey
wall will soar into the black
sky above it. With these
thoughts I await

what? what?
Whoever seeks to starve
my children and speaks words
of freedom will fall,
plummet. Shot in the throat

– 8 –

I try to rise, fall back
on my ass, urine
seeps on the floor;—there, there
it is again, My God!
so beautiful, visions
of fire, fire. This drink
cannot hold me, these streets
cannot hold me longer,
I will soar with the flames.

Red on black, I like that.
Lets hit the log, read the sparks.
My house is a scorched urn,
hopes for my children are embers.
I am drunk with joy.

– 9 –

pomme de reinette et pomme d'api ...
Emigration? Further
North? What job? What?
I know. I know you're cold.
There's only so many blankets.
Use my coat.
The deposit has to be certified.
The bank won't do it.
It's possible, if we don't eat.
Thank god for tea.
No, I haven't given up.
Yes, the leaves are beautiful.

I don't really know what's wrong.
They say the problem is overproduction.

geese stretch to rise, fall back
behind rushes, water
inflects dawn's sky;—there, there
they are again, My God
so beautiful, mist clears
as they rise. This bay
cannot hold them. These hills
cannot hold them longer.
They are formed in the sky.

I do not doubt, but neither
do I see them rise, drawn
with inward eyes, like the
V which falters mid-air.
There they are again, there!

BOOK TWO

Boethius has a vision in which he converses with Lady Philosophy

LADY PHILOSOPHY: What is hunger?

BOETHIUS: The habit of eating disturbed.

LADY PHILOSOPHY: And the hunger of your children?

BOETHIUS: The habit of their eating disturbed.

LADY PHILOSOPHY: Is that all?

BOETHIUS: They cry in the night. They chew paper.

LADY PHILOSOPHY: What is cold?

BOETHIUS: I don't know. What sort of question is that:
'What is cold?'?

LADY PHILOSOPHY: What are you doing?

BOETHIUS: Just listening. I'm listening to the sounds of the night. The children cling together like damp leaves, cold, hungry leaves on the floor, beneath my coat. They're okay.

LADY PHILOSOPHY: What do you hear?

BOETHIUS: The sound of the trees. The sound of the wind in the trees. A soft sound. Soughing.

LADY PHILOSOPHY: That's not the wind in the leaves. It's the slick of tires on pavement. The soughing of steel belted radials.

BOETHIUS: Don't you like it better as soughing boughs?

LADY PHILOSOPHY: Do you?

BOETHIUS: Almost the sound of trees. Almost the wind in the trees. Almost the soughing of boughs. The sweet soughing of an image that lies.

LADY PHILOSOPHY: The romantic image of nature.

BOETHIUS: That lies.

LADY PHILOSOPHY: What do you think of when I say the word "crop"?

BOETHIUS: A harvest.

LADY PHILOSOPHY: A happy choice, a harvest.

BOETHIUS: A real harvest. A real goddamn harvest, with real goddamn food. You?

LADY PHILOSOPHY: A horsewhip. I think of a horsewhip. A tool of control. A crop.

BOETHIUS: Can't you think of both, a harvest and a horsewhip?

LADY PHILOSOPHY:	You see the scars on my face? I did that with a razor blade. Thin white lines. Calligraphy on flesh.
BOETHIUS:	You're crazy.
LADY PHILOSOPHY:	Harvest and horsewhip, terms joined by the act of cutting. Nature and society joined by the act of cutting. The real meaning of crop is to cut.
BOETHIUS:	Crazy, crazy.
LADY PHILOSOPHY:	I am crazy. I'm crazy crazy. I'm crazy mad crazy. I'm crazy mad calligraphic crazy.
BOETHIUS:	I like the stretch of skin between your hips. I would like to put my hand there. Soft, but taut.
LADY PHILOSOPHY:	Do you want me to hold your head against my stomach?
BOETHIUS:	No
LADY PHILOSOPHY:	Do you want to feel my scars?
BOETHIUS:	No.
LADY PHILOSOPHY:	Thin lines between self-disgust and self-renewal. Thin, calligraphic lines. Cut. I cut them.
BOETHIUS:	You ever want to kill? To murder?
LADY PHILOSOPHY:	Yes.
BOETHIUS:	Who? Yourself?
LADY PHILOSOPHY:	No.
BOETHIUS:	Who?
LADY PHILOSOPHY:	Kufanele ukhuluma kahle.

BOETHIUS:	What does that mean?
LADY PHILOSOPHY:	It's in Zulu. My mother said that to me. She said it wasn't violence she supported but force, force to free herself from violence.
BOETHIUS:	Is that what it means?
LADY PHILOSOPHY:	No, it means 'say it correctly'. Kufanele ukhuluma kahle.
BOETHIUS:	I hear rain. Do you hear rain?
LADY PHILOSOPHY:	Or is it something else? Is it rain or the sound of teeth falling on the roof. You hear rain. I hear teeth falling on a metal roof.
BOETHIUS:	Before you came I went for a walk through the city with the children. I put them to bed. I read them my sonnets. I thought of suicide.
LADY PHILOSOPHY:	Does it help to think of death?
BOETHIUS:	Yes. I am an articulation of twigs: thin twigs in a thin wind, whining.
LADY PHILOSOPHY:	It's not really the image that consoles, but the act of lying which is a consolation.
BOETHIUS:	It helps to think of death, to contemplate death, then the desire for it seems as absurd as all other desires. I want to contemplate the images, the apparent order, until both pain and joy are mere facets, mere moments dissolving into an unsequenced night.
LADY PHILOSOPHY:	And the hunger of your children?
BOETHIUS:	This world is not a reflection of one's needs.
LADY PHILOSOPHY:	Precisely why desire exists.
BOETHIUS:	I … like the truth of ambivalent desires.

LADY PHILOSOPHY:	You hide in the hiding places of opposing meanings.
BOETHIUS:	I recognize contradictions. Nature works through contradiction.
LADY PHILOSOPHY:	Not logical contradiction, material contradictions, conflicts in the evolution of the material world.
BOETHIUS:	Nature itself has created the logical contradiction.
LADY PHILOSOPHY:	Only as a tool, to help construct the possible.
BOETHIUS:	The possible?
LADY PHILOSOPHY:	Given a choice between self-disgust and self renewal you call the night unsequenced and fade into an image.
BOETHIUS:	I am not a coward.
LADY PHILOSOPHY:	Aren't you?

BOOK THREE

Lady Philosophy recounts the story of Eurydice and thereby reveals her origins.

I am going to tell you the story of Orpheus.
Perhaps you know it already. You heard it
somewhere, saw it somewhere, scratched

on a toilet seat when you bent down with
your little straw, yes, the story of Orpheus,
the guy who loved his love so much that

he followed her to the dead, bringing her
to the sweet surface of life when oh my god
he looked back, breaking the agreement,

the charm, the whatever and she turned
into stone, salt, something dead, falling back
and once again he was alone without his love,

because, you see, he had looked back.
He was, shall we say, a bit of a reactionary.
And it cost. Oh my, did it cost.

I am the woman who was killed when Orpheus
looked back. I am that Eurydice. And I want to tell
his story, which is my story, which is our story.

Who was Orpheus? What was this guy really like?
Well, not surprising, first and foremost, he was a dealer.
I mean he dealt in illusions, was really good at it.

It came easy, natural, like the bank building glazed
in gold is natural. He had sweet substances which,
once in the veins, once, as an economist might put it,

in circulation, had a multiplier effect that put
compounding interest rates of even the worst
deregulated loan shark to shame, absolute shame,

verily I say unto you, pitiful shame. Upon consumption,
no, upon the mere scenting of vaporous odours which
lingered around the substances sweet singing Orpheus

peddled, the minds, let us call them that, of sullen buyers
reached for untold heights, absurd imaginings of sensual
pleasure, the tingling of flesh and the paroxysms of nerves

mounting to truly celestial heights, my God yes, even touching
the highest good, which is, for your information, at least a touch
higher than the World Trade Centre Twin buildings. Let us call it

a metaphysical height where fame, fortune, happiness
and power all fuse into a sweet song of sweet foreign
substances which, once scented, once administered,

once tendered, that's the word, tendered, and circulating
in the veins ... ah! I assure you, quite a song, quite a rush,
quite an investment with returns. What is he selling?

What is the nature of this highest good he proposes?
What is it within our historical epoch which will allow for you,
and your neighbour, and your neighbour's neighbour

to achieve happiness? What drug is this? I will tell you.
It is the future as a compounding percentage increase
of growing aggregate demand, all made possible by

an infinite growth of appropriate return on assets.
This is the illusion he is selling. Nothing can be better,
for all that is good and wise will flow from it.

Do you not believe it? Do you refuse this hot desire
from an ideological syringe? Will you not put on
the emerald tinted glasses and hold Dorothy's hand?

I assure you, this vision is guaranteed. Guaranteed
by who you may ask, by what, by ... wait for it ... read my lips,
guaranteed by the natural laws of reasonable return for those

who have something to wait for returns upon. All this
guaranteed, and read the smaller print, guaranteed by
natural laws of superior beings with, of course, it follows

naturally, superior assets, superior force. But how many
can refuse this sweet liquor of fantasy? In whose veins
is this ideological syringe not stuck? Through whose bodies

is the sickly sweetness not pumping and coursing? Such
illusions sweetly show in the expectant blush on the fresh
faces of the young Icarii called forth from beneath the back

porches where they giggled at their braces, called forth from
the courtyards of the schools where they walked the corridors
to awards of merit, called forth from their apprenticeships to poverty

paid for by the affluent mommies and daddies, called forth
and beyond that nonsense to their positions of almost power,
born aloft by the yellow puss of golden promises of a society

floating on ever returning returns: interest for all for all time;
fixed incomes built on ever sustained profit margins; play
while your money works; everything shining gleaming platinum.

"All we need," he sings, "is to cut the inefficiencies
from the system; your money deserves an honest return
for its work. And you, dear friend, have an untouched vein

aching for release. Soar with me and leave behind your
earthly cares." And as they soar, these young tomorrows,
it isn't the wings which melt, oh no, it's never never the wings

which melt, but the very flesh of their bodies as all their cells,
inmated by dreams of ultimate financial security, begin to drip,
the mutual fund certainty begins to drip, to drip the last tattered

remains of what was once young flesh. That sullied flesh is now
but dripping fat, an ocean of fat accumulating on the tired crust
of the beaten earth and this, this crusted layer of self-righteous

rancid fat, well-versed in the rhetoric of individual accomplishment,
well versed in the rhetoric of moral disguise, is the final resting place
for the once promising young Icarii, the best of their generation.

In bad shape? You could say that, but happy, oh yes, who
could conclude otherwise, for they have succeeded in believing
in the story to the bitter end, fallen brothers and sisters of the

heated spoon. But it is not that story that I tell, No, it is not the story
of the minor tragedies of the willfully duped, nor of how the pinpricks
of Orpheus twisted their sad and futile lives into a stupefying servitude

to the media icons of a video afterlife. No, the story I tell is of the visit
of this song-master to the underworld, and his search for me, Eurydice.
Because of the sweet harmonic weave of his honeyed voice Orpheus

was permitted to seek for his love among the dead. Yes, yes, it is true,
the gods wept with sadness when he sang of Eurydice, or perhaps
these cynical gods wept with the desire for sadness, or perhaps,

actually, were weeping with happiness at the possible mini-serial
to come out of it but, in any case, weep they did, and opened
the veins of time for the fixer to enter. So that he could seek

his love. So that he could seek his love. But who are the dead?
And where is Eurydice? Each year twelve million beneath the age
of five join the ranks, each month a million more, one every three

seconds, of dehydration, malnourishment. Where is Eurydice
among these masses? And who, in this underworld, does Orpheus
love, and what song will he sing?

> CHORUS:
>
> *Because of his sweet voice*
> *Orpheus was allowed to seek*
> *for his love among the dead.*
>
> *Yes, yes, it is true, the gods wept*
> *with sadness when he sang of Eurydice,*
> *or perhaps these more modern cynical gods*
>
> *wept with the desire for sadness, in any case*
> *they opened the veins of time*
> *for the fixer to enter. So that*
>
> *he could seek his love.*
> *But who are the dead?*
> *And where is Eurydice?*
>
> *Each year twelve million*
> *beneath the age of five join the ranks,*
> *each month a million more, one every*

three seconds, of dehydration, malnourishment.
Where is Eurydice among these masses?
And who, in this underworld, does Orpheus love,

and what song will he sing?

But now a short digression. Is my voice, raucous and untuned, not just the ignorance of the damned, the bitterness of a voice in retreat? Isn't the Berlin wall crumbling because Adam Smith

was not allowed across? Aren't dreams of utopia prostrate beneath the swelling multitudes clamouring for freedom in Eastern Europe? And dare we, can anyone dare, to criticize now the faultless flight

of capitalism, the invisible providence that rewards the worthy and dismisses the unequal; that lays the hands of supply and demand upon the heads of the kneeling supplicants, the divine hand,

for is not supply and demand the hand of providence, the will of a just and righteous god? And who now dares to deny that the white man in the golden Mercedes talking

on his phone is the archangel Michael? Who dares deny that as he calmly talks of the imperative of tight money policies he is not the voice of the angels? And verily, it is announced

by the Globe and Mail in a section of modern writing for the intelligent reader that this is the voice of the End of History, yes, the very End of History, for enmeshed

in the upholstery of the aforesaid golden Mercedes, and in all Mercedes, Porches, etc., there is the ultimate justice, and no one must question the fact that we, brothers and sisters, have arrived,

that the kingdom of god is upon us, and those who dare disagree are heretics of the worst order (so saith the Globe and Mail in the year 1989). Who dares question the End of History, calling this

imposing splendour a rancid crust of fat upon a shameful lie of well-being for all? Philosophy dares. The lovers of wisdom dare ask in whose service our services are rendered.

Thus endeth our digression.

Now, Orpheus triumphs in the underworld. In the land of shadows
his corpulence is impressive. The underworld elites, disciplined
by banker blue arias, feed broken biscuits to the thrice-headed

guard dogs of hell and Orpheus passes unscathed. Oh! The man
can sing! Puccini-like he sings of the International Monetary Fund.
Verdi-like he claps out the World Bank rag. What rationalizations

are not rhymed? There is a future if you do not disturb the giving
of appropriate returns on appropriate assets and the others can
labour in my new investments. Come children, I see you, I will

save you, follow me. And then he sees one, a child Beatrice
labouring in the fields, mines, factories, brothels of hell or
working not-at-all and he says, "My, my, my, how beautiful."

He sees the splendour of a breaking smile, the possibilities
of love and reason in the promising mauve of dawn, or is it
the haunted mauve of twilight, and he says: "Follow me."

And she does, and as long as he doesn't look back she will
be brought shining into the light, she too will be blessed but
if he looks back she will a shadow once more become. And

they are leaving the underworld, Orpheus and Eurydice,
haunting and beautiful melodies seep from the stones,
like veins of moss on rock the songs cling to the still air,

yes, see them, see them, the invisible chains of human love
pulled taut across the chasms of the living and the dead …

> CHORUS:
>
> *and at that moment he sees her,*
> *the beautiful Eurydice, the women he sought,*
> *he sees her, and says follow me*

and as long as he doesn't look back
she will be brought shining into the light,
she too will be blessed, but if he looks backs

she will a shadow once more become.
They are leaving the underworld,
Orpheus and Eurydice,

haunting and beautiful melodies seep
from the stones, like veins of moss
on rock the songs cling to the still air,

yes, see them, see them, the invisible chains
of human love pulled taut across the chasms
of the living and the dead

Now Orpheus, in this moment of glory, makes a choice.
He makes a choice, a premeditated choice. Orpheus chooses
to look back. He looks back and sings a song of regret, and sings

a song of tomorrow, and sings a song of eternal defeat in front
of impossible nature. For that is the crux of the Orpheus legend;
Orpheus, having succeeded in entering the underworld and finding

his so-called love, looks back. He looks back and sends millions
into the land of shade, starvation and death. And he says, "You
must understand, there is a deficit, your government cannot afford

medicine. (Although we will offer credits if you buy our arms
or other luxury items.)" And he says, "You must understand,
the price we used to pay for your commodities is too high,

they must be lower. (We can get a higher rate of return on
interest-bearing junk bonds.)" And he says, "You must understand,
you are a person without money or use, an inefficiency to be cut,

suffer little child and come not unto me. From you I cannot get
an appropriate return on assets, and that is the highest good. I saw
that you were beautiful, and that proves my humanity, I see

that there is no money to be made with you, and that proves
my wisdom. Fall back, Eurydice, and unto your image I will
be true. Fall back Eurydice, you are only dust."

And Eurydice, among the millions, one each breath,
fell back,
                and was dust.

Orpheus, of course, is quite impressed by the power of his voice.
And he draws, now, into his lungs, the fear of dying and the dust
of the dead. Replenished, for this is his replenishment, replenished,

he returns to the world above, humming a lullaby. In dust
there is neither reason nor love. The living, holding dust
on their palms, seeing dust in the air, neither hold reason

nor see love, and are afraid. And among the living, with
neither reason nor love, there can only be fear, and fear,
at last we say it, fear is the essential ingredient of the sweet

potent perfumes of his songs. Not greed, but fear. Not
ignorance, but fear. Fear is the rush of Orpheus' fix.
It is fear that he is calling the highest good. And as Orpheus

hums his lullaby so those falling asleep are legion. They sleep,
and yet are afraid. And in their fearful sleep they chant, they
repeatedly chant that all policies of the golden Mercedes are

the policies of God at the very end of history. And I am that
Beatrice, who found through deception my true name, Eurydice,
and who speaks now as Philosophy, for Philosophy belongs

to those who are deceived, and know their deception. And
I am that Beatrice, who found through deception my true name,
Eurydice, and who speaks, who speaks, now, as Lady Philosophy,

for Philosophy belongs to those who are deceived and know
their deception. And I ... I ... I know my deception, I that am
Bea Bea Beatrice trice, trice, who, who found through, through,

deception my name, my name, I now Eurydice, now as Philo,
Phil, Ph Ph for longs, philosophy longs, who, who, deceived,
I I I that speaks now no names knowing deception am, sp sp

speak, speak, speaking I I I Ph ph ph who found, who found
phil phil I phil found I I knowing deception falling one a breath
in the dust I Beatrice Eurydice now am speaking for

BOOK FOUR

Boethius tries to talk to The Chorus

CHORUS: The wind is dying.
             The wind is dead.
             The world is cold.
             Is he lame?

BOETHIUS: No, I am not lame, merely hurt.

CHORUS: Is he a beggar?

BOETHIUS: No, I am not a beggar, merely poor.

CHORUS: Ah! Not lame?

EURYDICE: Hurt.

CHORUS: Not a beggar?

EURYDICE: Poor.

CHORUS: The wind is dying.
             The wind is dead.

BOETHIUS: The air is thinned with cold.

CHORUS: Does he hear the madwoman?
             Does he hear the cry of the madwoman?

EURYDICE: He hears something.

CHORUS: C'est une femme, elle pleure.
            C'est une fille, elle pleure.
            Elles pleurent ensemble, les filles qui meurent,
            Les femmes qui voient les filles qui meurent.
            Elles pleurent ensemble.

BOETHIUS: A soft sound, soft. A soughing.

EURYDICE: The dead child is put to the breast
            of a dying woman. The sun burns.

BOETHIUS: I am cold. Is there something,
            a mutant something that cries in despair?

CHORUS: A travers les pleurs de temps les voix
            des muets nous parviennent, lentement

BOETHIUS: Who are they?

CHORUS: Qui demande qui pleure?

EURYDICE: I ask.

CHORUS: Qui demande qui pleure?

EURYDICE: I ask.

CHORUS: Les mots des muets nous parviennent, lentement.

EURYDICE: I have cut the question
            into my flesh, and rubbed
            ash in the cut so the scars
            would stay. I dare ask.

CHORUS: Qui demande qui pleure.

EURYDICE: I ask.

CHORUS: The words of the silenced cannot be heard.

EURYDICE: I am Eurydice.

CHORUS: Eurydice is dead.
             She is among us
             and cannot return.

EURYDICE: I am the question that asks
             what the silenced speak.

CHORUS: With whom are you walking?

EURYDICE: He seeks consolation.

CHORUS: Ah! A philosopher.

EURYDICE: He is full of self-loathing and defeat.

CHORUS: Ah! A coward.

BOETHIUS: The cries of my children haunt me.
             I do not know if they are alive or dead.

CHORUS: Has he killed his children?

EURYDICE: They are hungry.

CHORUS: Ha ha, ha ha ha,
             Ha ha ha ha ha ha,
             Ha ha, ha ha ha
             Let him seek life,
             and not descend
             among us.

BOETHIUS: Beatrice!

CHORUS: Eurydice!

BOETHIUS: Beatrice!

CHORUS: Her hand is in the fire of dawn. She burns.
             Her tongue is in the fire of dusk. She burns.
             She is dead and cannot return.

BOETHIUS:	Eurydice!
CHORUS:	Eurydice! Eurydice!
BOETHIUS:	Revolt. Compassion. Compassion. Revolt. This is a naked landscape. One word signifies another.
CHORUS:	Les voix des muets nous parviennent, lentement les voix nous parviennent a travers Ha ha ha ha ha ha, ha ha ha ha ha ha, ha ha ha ha ha ha.

BOOK FIVE

Boethius and Lady Philosophy try and succeed to speak together.

BOETHIUS:	I imagined a chorus which said that consolation is not possible, unless on the path of compassion, unless on the road of revolt.
LADY PHILOSOPHY:	Imagine a compassion which extends to the strong, as well as to the weak, to the rich as well as to the poor, to the guilty as well as to the innocent, to the torturer as well as to the tortured.
BOETHIUS:	Among the dead and was raising her from the dead, bringing her to the sweet surface of life when oh my god he looked back and

LADY PHILOSOPHY:	Is it possible? Is it revolt? Or no revolt at all? Is it possible as other than a state of self-renunciation? As other than that?
BOETHIUS:	I don't know. Predicate the possibility. Discover the determinants.
LADY PHILOSOPHY:	Let evil be rewarded by unhappiness; let virtue be rewarded by delights.
BOETHIUS:	To an extent, in my own life, but not in the world, not in the world. There is only the pretence of symmetry between a conscience and a society.
BOTH:	They are not the same thing.
BOETHIUS:	If there is neither a belief in compassion, nor in revolt, there is no need of consolation.
BOTH:	Once upon a time there was a god, one god, birthed, perhaps, of a great search for compassion, birthed, perhaps, of a great search for revolt, predicated, perhaps, upon the mysteries of logical necessity,
LADY PHILOSOPHY:	And the sequences of our lives became a simultaneity. Pain and joy merely
BOETHIUS:	image upon image in an unsequenced night.
LADY PHILOSOPHY:	And given an unsequenced night, causality itself is a perception
BOETHIUS:	The fossil is aesthetic, I am aesthetic, a fossil, smooth beneath the tongue, god such … two hands so, I know, I know she's cold, there's only so many blankets …

LADY PHILOSOPHY: Causality merely the etched trace
                    of a failed morality. Our history.
                    Ah Boethius! What need, what great need
                    to postulate that construction,
                    the ideal idealized

BOETHIUS: This bay cannot hold us longer.
                    We are formed in the sky.

LADY PHILOSOPHY: And leave and leave the rest of the world
                    leave it the world, leave it alone lonely
                    path virtue leaving it

BOETHIUS: The fossil is aesthetic I am aesthetic a fossil
                    smooth beneath the tongue, god, such …
                    There are only so many blankets …

LADY PHILOSOPHY: interpretation rooted/history
                    history rooted/interpretation

BOETHIUS: The facades crumble, the possible,
                    constructed, crumbles under the same
                    great need as defined it,
                    no longer one coherence.
                    Then identity? Who dares ask?
                    No cuts on my face.
                    Some useful sense, perhaps,
                    identity as capacity to effect change
                    within the sets of possible worlds:
                    loss of identity, the inability
                    to effect change,
                    the loss of possible worlds.
                    I don't know what's wrong.
                    They say the problem is over-production.

LADY PHILOSOPHY: So let us call morality a dialectic of fiction
and need, storytelling and sorrow.
Let us call it, at best, an appropriate evasion,
spoken at inappropriate moments.

BOETHIUS: There was a time when the mutual
recognition of many narrators seemed
possible. Universal revolt. Humanism.

LADY PHILOSOPHY: Ah! There was a time,
a blessed time, soon to be, soon
the mass revolt, the revolt of the masses,
wherein identity, etched in struggle.

BOETHIUS: Let us now call morality a dialectic
of fiction and need,
storytelling and sorrow.
Let us now call it that.

BOTH: We remember the ancient voices,
the cries of the silenced, dim choruses,
the many I's, deceived, and deceiving.
We hear the beating wings.
Not despair through lack of faith;
that would be easy, a simple lack of faith,
but despair of the means itself,
after the cut of absolute morality,
after the soughing of historical inevitability.

BOETHIUS: Material slash interpretation, nature
and society joined by the act of cutting.
The harvest: deception knows deception
wherein philosophy dares and dares again.
Once there was a compassionate god,
Once the winds of inherent progress,

| BOTH: | Carry the harvest.
Our trip to the dead
ends with the living.
We know our own deception.
And here philosophy is reborn.
It dares.
For we and our children
are not unworthy of life,
our poverty the proof. |
|---|---|
| BOETHIUS: | The path well travelled becomes the road.
Compassion to revolt is a question of use. |

FREEPORT, TEXAS

———

CAST

(In order of appearance)

BEN: Late 50's, on top of his game as a corporate president.
RICHARD: Accountant, early 40's.
MONICA: Ben's adventurous daughter, late 20's.
HOLLY: Monica's mother, Ben's wife.
IVAN: Russian, late-20's.
FLORA: Late 30's, long time executive assistant to Richard.
PAUL: Mid to late 40's. Ben's right hand man.
MIKE: Manager at an exotic dance club, mid to late 30's,
LERA: Mid 20's, an exotic dancer. Originally from Russia.
NORA: Older woman, living in a small cabin on stilts on the beach.

ACT ONE

SCENE ONE

A Social for the Senior Executives and their partners: dancing, music, and interwoven conversations.

BEN: Richard, Richard! Glad you're here.

RICHARD: You did invite the senior staff.

BEN: And it's a very good turnout.

RICHARD: We do as our new President bids.

BEN: People want to belong to a company that's alive and kicking. We celebrate or die.

RICHARD: These are not my favorite events.

BEN: Motivation is everything.

RICHARD: Motivation?

BEN: Yes.

RICHARD: Not profits?

BEN: Without motivation, there are no profits. Do you mind if I broach something personal?

RICHARD: Please.

BEN: I don't want you as our Comptroller anymore.

RICHARD: No?

BEN: I want you as our Chief Financial Officer.

RICHARD: I'm stunned.

BEN: Can't you do the job?

RICHARD: I am the best person for it.

BEN: Then why the surprise?

RICHARD: I thought you would bring in one of your own.

BEN: You have integrity, expertise, the loyalty of
            everyone here. You are the man.

RICHARD: The man?

BEN: If you accept.

RICHARD: Ben, may I call you Ben?

BEN: Of course.

RICHARD: Your group bought control at a premium. You are
            carrying a pretty serious debt.

BEN: Agreed.

RICHARD: And this company is efficiently run.

BEN: Efficient, yes, but not imaginative.

RICHARD: What do you imagine, splitting the company,
            selling the pieces?

BEN: No, no. Nothing like that.

RICHARD: So where are the profits to service the debt?

BEN: Richard, I hire the right people to make the right
            decisions. Are you interested?

RICHARD: Do I have your confidence?

BEN: Yes.

RICHARD: I am tempted.

BEN: Good. We can discuss the details later.

RICHARD: I would appreciate that.

BEN: Ah, Holly, I was about to look for you. Holly, Monica, this is Richard, our new CFO.

RICHARD: It's a pleasure to meet you.

HOLLY: Are you enjoying the evening, Richard?

RICHARD: Yes, I am.

MONICA: It's a bit like a goldfish bowl, isn't it? Everyone swims in circles and nods at each other, and the hors d'oeuvres are little flakes of food falling from the sky.

BEN: Is that how you see it?

HOLLY: Well, what's wrong with being a fish, as long as the water is clean?

BEN: I wouldn't want to be a fish.

HOLLY: Would you object, Richard?

RICHARD: It's not my first choice.

HOLLY: They say we were all fish once, I mean, we were spawned in the oceans.

MONICA: They have short memories.

BEN: Who?

MONICA: Fish. I don't know how exactly, but they've timed how long a goldfish can hold a memory. Two seconds. Imagine. Two seconds. They don't have enough memory to get bored. They swim in their bowl and every time they turn they say to themselves: Look, a castle! *(two second pause)* Look, a castle!

RICHARD: Can they do that, measure the length of a memory?

MONICA: Do you remember my name, Richard?

RICHARD: Your name?

MONICA: When my father introduced us he told it to you.

RICHARD: No, I'm sorry. I don't think I heard it clearly.

MONICA: Well, I'll do a turn of the room and when I come back we can be introduced again. (*To* Ben) Take care of your wife.

BEN: I always do.

MONICA: She is my mother.

BEN: I remember.

Monica leaves them

RICHARD: She's engaging.

BEN: You could say that. Three times in fact she's been engaged and has broken it off.

HOLLY: She was right every time.

BEN: May we continue our conversation tomorrow?

RICHARD: The details, where the devil hides.

Monica approaches Ivan.

MONICA: So, who are you? A Director of Marketing, a Market Analyst, a Vice President of Something Somewhere?

IVAN: No, I'm nobody. Well, not nobody, a Russian, on loan from my company at home.

MONICA: A Russian?

IVAN: I am supposed to learn from the experts. So, here I am, Houston.

MONICA: You speak English well.

IVAN:	I have been speaking English since I was a child.
MONICA:	Do you like Texas?
IVAN:	I'm impressed by the air conditioning. Everywhere you go it's freezing, even in the middle of the hottest day.
MONICA:	We used to be frightened of you Russians. When we were kids we thought you wanted to bomb us all to hell. Nuke us. But now we treat you like children, display you like toys. Which do you prefer? Being feared, or being patronized?
IVAN:	Is that the choice?
MONICA:	I don't think anybody here sees an alternative.
IVAN:	This room is full of intelligent people, you underestimate them.

Ben and Holly have left Richard, Flora approaches Richard

FLORA:	And?
RICHARD:	You're talking to the new CFO, Flora.
FLORA:	Congratulations.
RICHARD:	I didn't expect it. I didn't.
FLORA:	No-one has worked harder.
RICHARD:	Except maybe you.
FLORA:	It's called teamwork.
RICHARD:	And I am grateful.
FLORA:	What's the new boss like?
RICHARD:	Insightful, a good judge of character. Picks his men well, don't you think?

Monica and Ivan are still talking

MONICA: I am going to touch your lips with my finger. Like this. Now tell me. Do you want to bite my hand or lick my fingers?

IVAN: Why are you doing this?

MONICA: To see if you want me to fear you, or to pet you.

IVAN: I can't tell you what I want.

MONICA: Aaah!

IVAN: What?

MONICA: Now I know.

IVAN: I didn't say anything.

MONICA: Do you see that man over there?

IVAN: Which one?

MONICA: The ugly one, well, that's no help, they are all ugly, each in his own peculiar way. That one.

IVAN: Yes.

MONICA: I am attracted to him.

IVAN: Why?

MONICA: I was talking to him and he didn't notice my existence.

IVAN: You like that?

MONICA: He's free. I chase freedom.

IVAN: Maybe you're attracted to indifference?

MONICA: Oooh … I'll have to think about that.

Paul approaches Ben.

PAUL: I saw you speaking to Richard.

BEN: I thought we had a good conversation.

PAUL: I hope he joins us. The analysts love him.

BEN: We made some headway. Who is that leaving with my daughter?

Monica says something in Ivan's ear. They begin to leave.

PAUL: In the finance department, a Russian.

BEN: What does he do?

PAUL: Econometrics. You know, bullshit numbers generated by bullshit computer programs that forecast demand.

BEN: That's a bit dismissive, Paul.

PAUL: I'm not an academic, Ben.

BEN: Do you think he has designs on her?

PAUL: Why not, she's attractive.

BEN: Then pity him. No one takes advantage of my Monica.

SCENE TWO

Monica leads Ivan into an erotic dance club.

IVAN: This is a strange place to bring me.

MONICA: Isn't it what you want?

IVAN: No. I wanted to go to some quiet place where you and I could talk.

MONICA: I can get a girl to dance just for you. Watch.

IVAN: Don't. You know, they have this at home.

MONICA: It is rather basic. But you men, you like that.

IVAN: Are you trying to tease me?

MONICA: No, that's what I'm not doing.

IVAN: I don't want to be here.

MONICA: No?

IVAN: No.

MONICA: Too bad. You might be more interesting if you did.

Mike, the manager, joins them.

MIKE: Monica! Couldn't get you to change your mind and
            come back, could I? Always need a good girl.

MONICA: God alone knows what you mean by "good".

MIKE: Who's your handsome friend?

MONICA: A very nice but serious Russian. Will you take care
            of him?

MIKE: A lot of our girls come from over there. They
            speak Romanian, Ukrainian, Bulgarian, Albanian,
            Russian, all sorts of funny languages.

IVAN: We were just about to leave.

MIKE: Don't do that. I'll find a Ruskie for you.

Mike hurries away.

IVAN: You used to work here?

MONICA: You have something against physical labor?

IVAN:	Did you need the money?
MONICA:	I needed the experience.

Mike returns with Lera in tow. She is wearing cowboy boots and a Stetson. Monica melts away.

MIKE:	Valeria, say hello to your countryman.
LERA:	Привет. (Hi.)
IVAN:	Привет. Я не хочу быть здесь. (Hi. I don't want to be here.)
LERA:	Почему нет? (Why not?)
IVAN:	Я не хочу тебя обидеть. (I don't mean to offend you.)
MIKE:	What did he say?
LERA:	He wants to know what I'm doing here.
IVAN:	That's not what I said.
MIKE:	She's supposed to be dancing.

Lera starts to dance and Mike leaves.

IVAN:	Who is that guy?
LERA:	Mike.
IVAN:	What does he do?
LERA:	He takes care of us.
IVAN:	Is he good at it?
LERA:	He's very good at it.
IVAN:	Where did the woman go? The one I came in with?
LERA:	Monica?

IVAN:	Yes.
LERA:	She left.
IVAN:	She wouldn't leave without me.
LERA:	She just did. Do you want me to keep dancing?
IVAN:	I didn't choose to come here, she brought me.
LERA:	*(Laughs)* Against your will?
IVAN:	You don't believe me?
LERA:	You have to pay like anyone else, dollars, not rubles.
IVAN:	Where are you from?
LERA:	Novokuznetsk.
IVAN:	It seems strange, someone from Novokuznetsk dancing for me in Houston.
LERA:	You can pretend I'm from California.

SCENE THREE

Same evening, Holly's bedroom. Ben is with her.

HOLLY:	Look at my body. It is a good body for a fifty year old who drinks too much. Not perfect, but good.
BEN:	You spend enough money on it.
HOLLY:	I see. If that's the case, then what's your excuse, a lack of funds?
BEN:	Was that wit?
HOLLY:	Are you angry because I drank? I had the tiniest bit. Just a tickle. I didn't embarrass you, did I?
BEN:	No. You were very good.

HOLLY:	I had fun.
BEN:	I'm glad.
HOLLY:	Come over here and hold me.
BEN:	You need coffee.
HOLLY:	I don't need coffee. I want a hug. *(He hugs her, briefly)* Thank you.
BEN:	Don't thank me. I can't stand that.
HOLLY:	I'm sorry.
BEN:	Don't apologize.
HOLLY:	No, never.
BEN:	I didn't hug you as a favor.
HOLLY:	No, as a responsibility. As a duty. Do you have any regrets in your life?
BEN:	Of course I do.
HOLLY:	I have none.
BEN:	*(Laughs with surprise)* Not one?
HOLLY:	I used to. The list was as long as my arm. But now, at this moment, not one. I love you and that makes me happy.
BEN:	I love you.
HOLLY:	You don't believe that. You say it to make me happy, but you don't believe it. And yet, I know that you do … love me.
BEN:	You know me better than I know myself?
HOLLY:	Yes. Definitely. And I don't regret anything because I know that there is this love between us. To love, and to be loved, what more is there?

BEN: You should sleep.

HOLLY: Will you pray with me?

BEN: No.

Ben goes to leave the room

HOLLY: Don't go. Listen to my prayer. I want you to hear it.

BEN: Holly …

HOLLY: Dear God … *(To Ben)* Please listen to me. Dear
          God, whatever you are, wherever you are …

BEN: Whatever you are, now that's a convincing start …

HOLLY: Let Ben hear your voice, and feel your presence.

BEN: Jesus, Holly …

HOLLY: Forgive me my weaknesses and forgive Ben his. We
          are weak, and know that we need your strength.
          We know that without you we are lost as infant
          babes. Guide us, Lord, so that we may see your path
          clearly, and that we may walk on it with purpose,
          and generosity, and maybe even a little dignity.

BEN: Amen.

HOLLY: Amen.

BEN: I liked the dignity part. I, too, would ask for
          dignity if I was half dressed, half drunk, on my
          knees and talking to something, I'm not sure what,
          which may or may not be listening.

HOLLY: Don't be cruel.

BEN: You turn to God because you don't get fucked enough.

HOLLY: God is there to be found, that's what's important,
          not why we look.

BEN: Is that so?

HOLLY: I have an idea, Ben. Take it as a challenge, fuck me
          more often and see if I still believe.

BEN: You confuse me, Holly.

HOLLY: Come here. Let me hold you. You need me as
          much as I need you. Don't you know that?

BEN: No.

HOLLY: You think that something better is waiting for
          you around the corner, you've always thought that.
          A better car, a better house, and admit it, a better
          wife, just around the next corner. Younger, prettier,
          smarter …

BEN: That might be nice.

HOLLY: But I love you, Ben, and you love me. That's what
          confuses you, you love me, and still you wait for
          someone better. You can't accept life the way it is.
          You just can't.

BEN: You seem to believe what you're saying.

HOLLY: I am sure of it.

BEN: It's just a technique, Holly. I do that in my work all
          the time.

HOLLY: Do what?

BEN: Speak with conviction so that others agree. Speak
          in such a way that doubt isn't possible.

HOLLY: Is that what you think I am doing—I want to con
          you into loving me?

BEN: I didn't mean that.

HOLLY: I think you did.

BEN:	Good night, Holly.
HOLLY:	Open your heart, Ben.

SCENE FOUR

Flora enters Richard's office.

FLORA:	The President wants to see you.
RICHARD:	Arrange a time.
FLORA:	He thinks now would be good.
RICHARD:	Not now, I have a conference call with the brokers.
FLORA:	I told him. He wants you to postpone the call.
RICHARD:	Postpone it? Now? On such short notice? They'll think we have a crisis in the company. We can't do that. Unless there is a crisis?
FLORA:	I imagine he'll tell you.
RICHARD:	All right. All right. Tell the brokers that the call has been postponed until, I don't know. Christ, I don't do this kind of thing! It's unprofessional. Just … Handle it, Flora. You'll know what to do.

Richard exits his office and then enters the conference room.
Ben enters last.

BEN:	Good.
RICHARD:	Can't we have this meeting a bit later?
BEN:	We only have one agenda item, this won't take long.
RICHARD:	Does it have to be now?

BEN:	Of course it has to be now. That's why I called it now. I don't want anyone talking to brokers, journalists, the competition, their wives, their girlfriends, whoever, until we all get straight our response to the upcoming announcement.
RICHARD:	Announcement?
BEN:	If you'd just listen for a moment—the White House is going to approve a deregulated energy market.
RICHARD:	That's just a tired rumor!
PAUL:	It was, but it's time has come.
RICHARD:	What's changed? Why now? How can they say yes now?
PAUL:	Every administration needs re-election funds.
BEN:	What are you trying to say, Paul?
PAUL:	I am praising the dynamics of a healthy democracy.
RICHARD:	How can they deregulate in a monopoly situation?
BEN:	This administration is willing to stick to its principles, and a competitive economy is one of them.
PAUL:	You may assume that we have made a certain commitment to expressing our gratitude.
BEN:	That's not the issue. Not at all.
RICHARD:	When is this announcement supposed to be made?
PAUL:	Mid-afternoon.
BEN:	Which brings me to the point—our response. *(He takes out a piece of paper, and reads from it.)* We welcome this opportunity to compete in a free market. While prices may go up in the short term, its only part of the cycle. We will not

meet our competition lying down. We will invest
aggressively, creating new jobs, new ideas. We will
innovate today for energy security tomorrow.

RICHARD: I take it that's our message.

BEN: And I would like the analysts to hear it.

RICHARD: I understand.

BEN: To hear it, and to believe it.

RICHARD: I can get them to listen.

BEN: I want them to believe.

PAUL: The brokers get a cut from every trade. They won't
              need a lot of persuasion.

BEN: Everyone can make money on this. It's a win-win
              situation. The brokers, the investors, the company,
              the country. And that's the message to deliver.
              Win-win for everyone. They'll believe, Richard,
              if you believe.

RICHARD: Innovation today for energy security tomorrow.

BEN: That's the ticket. Have Flora reschedule the call. Lean
              forward and don't give them an inch. You don't need
              a lot of particulars. Just stick to the general thrust.

Richard leaves.

BEN: Can he convince them?

PAUL: He'll be fine.

BEN: How do you know?

PAUL: It's in his character to succeed. It's all he really knows.

BEN: Maybe. I want to speak to him alone. *(Ben exits and catches up to Richard)* I just wanted to catch you for a second and ask if you were enjoying your new position.

RICHARD: Enjoy? That's not the word I would use. I feel that everything is moving too quickly.

BEN: Richard, do the best you can, but know that no-one expects you to do the impossible.

RICHARD: I'm glad to hear you say that.

BEN: I have a favor to ask. I had promised my wife and daughter that I'd sail with them this week-end, but I can't find time. Would you go instead?

RICHARD: They won't want me as your replacement.

BEN: They might. It drives them crazy that I sail with a cellphone to one ear.

RICHARD: I've never sailed.

BEN: No? Well, all the more reason.

RICHARD: I've often wanted to.

BEN: The Gulf of Mexico is a beautiful place on a sunny day.

RICHARD: They won't mind me stumbling about on deck? I won't have to climb the topmast and haul sail?

BEN: The boat almost steers itself. It's not exactly primitive.

RICHARD: I'd love to go.

BEN: Bring good sunglasses, a hat, and lots of sunblock. You'll enjoy it. The wind, the waves. The wind, the waves, the waves, the waves. It's a bit repetitive but a nice way to relax. Don't bring your phone.

SCENE FIVE

Holly, Monica and Richard are on a sailing boat.

RICHARD: Is it deep here?

MONICA: It's over your head.

RICHARD: I knew that.

MONICA: We could do with a bit more wind.

RICHARD: It would be hard to imagine a more perfect day.

MONICA: The wind will pick up. We just have to go further out.

RICHARD: It doesn't get better than this.

MONICA: Really? You can't imagine anything better?

RICHARD: Well, I mean …

MONICA: Wait until we get out a bit. Then you'll see what sailing is really like. You'll be flying over the waves.

HOLLY: My daughter worships speed. A fast ride is the best she can imagine.

MONICA: This boat is designed to race. Why are we here, if that's not what we want?

(The boom sweeps the boat and they duck to take up new positions.)

SCENE SIX

Lera and Ivan are on the beach in Freeport.

LERA: I think it was here. It's hard for me to tell.

IVAN: You gave birth lying here, on the beach?

LERA: I was in a van. We were trying to make it to a
           doctor in Galveston. But I knew the baby was
           coming too fast. I was trying to tell the driver to
           stop. She would look at me with her wide eyes and
           then just speed up. I wanted her to help me, not to
           drive like a maniac while I gave birth in the back. I
           reached between my legs and I could feel the top of
           my baby's head. Then I really screamed. She finally
           understood. She pulled off the road and drove right
           onto the beach. She ran to the side of the van and
           pushed open the sliding door. The fresh air hit me
           and I just sucked it in. Salty. I remember looking
           out and I couldn't tell where the water stopped and
           the sky started. Everything was a haze, a kind of
           mauve. The baby was pushing out of me and I was
           in this strange country with a strange woman on a
           strange beach and I couldn't tell up from down.

IVAN: Were you frightened?

LERA: I had no time to be frightened. I didn't care about
           anything other than wanting to push. The driver
           stood between my legs, blowing out her breath
           in a pattern. I knew that she wanted me to breath
           like her, to copy her, but I couldn't. I was being
           split apart. One hand held the headrest and the
           other where the seat belt joins the frame. Then,
           oh my God, a terrible, terrible moment of silence.
           Please, let there be a sound, some sound from the
           baby. Probably that lasted only half a minute or
           so but I thought it was forever, and then I heard
           the driver groan and spit and my baby started to
           cry and I couldn't help it, I started to cry, tears just
           burst out of me and the driver started to laugh and
           cry, both. She was saying something in Spanish, I
           started to yell something in Russian, and then she
           put my little baby into my arms and I held her on

my chest. My God, the whole world was living and breathing and crying on my chest.

IVAN: On this beach?

LERA: She had sucked the mucous from my baby's nose with her mouth and spat it out. She had used her shoelace to tie the umbilical cord. Then she massaged my uterus until she was sure that everything was out. Somehow she knew that.

IVAN: I wouldn't know that.

LERA: My baby was bloody and her nose was pushed to one side and the top of her head met in a strange point and she was the most beautiful person I had ever seen. I looked out the open door and it was becoming purple all around, the purple of almost night except above the very edge of the sea, where I could see a thin sliver of golden horizon, a faint light that seemed to circle the earth and hold it together. Then this women, this strange women whom I had never met until that day took my baby from me. She took her from me very gently and walked right into the water and bathed her. I struggled to sit up and watch from the van, but it had become too dark to see anything. I could hear her, and she started to sing softly and I knew it was fine, that my baby was as safe with her as with me. And I never saw that woman again, I don't know her name or where she lives. Do you ever wish you were a woman?

IVAN: Sometimes I wish I wasn't myself. But that's not what you mean.

LERA: To be a woman to give birth? All of a sudden you realize that on this planet, among all the fucked up adults, there are little people, smelling of milk, deserving to live.

IVAN: Do you want to go back?

LERA: Not right away. Not yet. Let's climb into that cabin.
            It reminds me of Siberia, on stilts like that.

SCENE SEVEN

*The wind is picking up. The boom again sweeps across the deck
and all move to the other side, where they lean back, pulling hard
against the ropes, holding the sails taut.*

MONICA: Keep the line taut! Use your weight!

RICHARD: How?

MONICA: Lean back!

RICHARD: I don't know how!

HOLLY: He doesn't know what to do!

MONICA: Lean! Like this!

RICHARD: It can't be safe!

MONICA: What? You have to speak up.

HOLLY: He wants to know if it's safe!

RICHARD: I didn't mean that!

MONICA: Lean! Go on, lean!

*Richard stands and leans back over the edge of the boat. The sound
of the wind and the waves is quite loud.*

RICHARD: Amazing!

MONICA: Don't you want to scream into the wind?

RICHARD: What?

MONICA:	Scream? Into the wind?
RICHARD:	I can't hear you!
MONICA:	It's fantastic. I love this.

SCENE EIGHT

Lera and Ivan open an unlocked door. An old lady sits in a chair by the window of the single room.

NORA:	Should I phone the police, or just shoot you?
IVAN:	We didn't know anybody was here.
NORA:	Where's my gun? I had a gun here somewhere.
LERA:	It was my idea, I'm sorry.
IVAN:	We're leaving.
NORA:	That's a good idea, a dandy idea. But before you do, you wouldn't happen to have a cigarette on you?
IVAN:	I do. Yes. Can I give you one?
NORA:	Well, how about that!
IVAN:	Here. Take the pack.
NORA:	The pack! A full pack! Oh, it is my lucky day. You never know when blessings will descend. The world is strange that way.
IVAN:	Would you like a light?
NORA:	No, I don't smoke.
IVAN:	So why did you ask for a cigarette?

NORA: Every time I take a cigarette away from someone I feel virtuous. And if I can take a whole pack I feel very virtuous. A good day.

IVAN: You can't do that. You can't have them if you're not going to smoke them. Give them back!

NORA: Tough. Pollutes your lungs, pollutes the air.

LERA: Do you live here?

NORA: Have nowhere else. I should be calling the President, tell him I have some strange people poking around for state secrets down on the beach in Freeport.

IVAN: I doubt if there are state secrets here.

NORA: God damn right there are! Every dead fish, every mutant shrimp, all the waste from the chemical companies, every sulphur fume. Texas is chock-a-block full of state secrets! We are proud to have the biggest state secrets in the Union!

LERA: I don't think you should call anyone. Please.

NORA: All right, you ask nice like that and I won't. Besides, I'd be embarrassed if I phoned and no-one would listen. I wouldn't like that. It would make me feel small. Supposing I actually had a phone, which I don't.

LERA: You have a wonderful view.

NORA: The best there is. Nothing but what God gave us, oh, and that itsy-bitsy sailboat that thinks it's winning some race.

LERA: Have you lived here a long time?

NORA: Not too long. Thirty years. Every day I've looked
           out this window, every day it's the same and yet
           different. Do you want me to tell you your future?

LERA: Can you do that?

NORA: You'll have to pay for it.

IVAN: Do you sit here with no sign, lights off, and wait
           for the wind to blow customers in? Preferably
           customers that smoke.

NORA: You can pay me whatever you want, just make sure
           you think it adequate to the occasion. I like that
           phrase, adequate to the occasion.

IVAN: All right.

NORA: We can do this a couple of ways. We can have tea
           and I'll read the tea leaves. That's kind of a classic.
           Or, if you want, we can do it with a deck of cards.
           I guess that's kind of a classic, too.

LERA: I'd like the tea.

NORA: Ran out of tea.

LERA: Then the cards.

NORA: I don't have the full deck anymore. You know,
           some swear by the divination of sacrificed animals.
           Another kind of classic. You kill the animal, open
           it up, muck about a bit with the insides, and then
           tell the future. That adds a certain, what's the word,
           gravitas to the ceremony. But it makes no difference
           what you use if you have the gift, and if you don't
           have the gift killing animals isn't going to help. But
           it keeps certain customers happy. Some customers
           like the gravitas. But I like it simple. Here, girl,
           hold my hands. I'll get everything I need from your
           fingers. *(They hold hands)* You have a child.

LERA:	One.
NORA:	Does your child have any problems?
LERA:	No.
NORA:	A daughter?
LERA:	Yes. How did you know that?
NORA:	Not really a lot of choice, either a boy or a girl.
IVAN:	Do you need to hold her hands?
NORA:	I need to feel her fingers.
IVAN:	You're asking questions about the present, not telling her about the future.
NORA:	That's the whole trick.
LERA:	Don't stop.
NORA:	You love your child.
LERA:	I love my child.
NORA:	Of course.

Nora is suddenly upset and withdraws her hands.

LERA:	What did you see?
NORA:	Nothing. I saw nothing.
LERA:	You saw something. I felt it. Your hands jumped.
NORA:	You love your daughter. That's good.
LERA:	Why can't you tell me?
NORA:	A strange image, that's all.
LERA:	You have to tell me.

NORA:	I don't have to do anything. Go away. Get out! Is that clear? Get out of here!
LERA:	I'll come back.

SCENE NINE

Flora enters Richard's office.

FLORA:	Can I talk to you?
RICHARD:	Of course.
FLORA:	You're angry. Most days, now, you are angry.
RICHARD:	I am trying to succeed in a very difficult position.
FLORA:	Do you have to be ruthless to those around you?
RICHARD:	I am adapting to my circumstances.
FLORA:	You can talk to me, Richard.
RICHARD:	What are you hoping I will say?
FLORA:	Whatever is on your mind. We have always spoken the truth to each other. You can count on me for that.
RICHARD:	We are friends. We can say intimate things. We don't have to worry about consequences.
FLORA:	That's right.
RICHARD:	Talk without reservation?
FLORA:	No reservation.
RICHARD:	All right. I want his daughter. I want her to come to me of her own free will. I want her, Flora. I can hardly think of anything else. It plagues me.
FLORA:	I didn't expect you to say that.

RICHARD: I know.

FLORA: Why? Why her?

RICHARD: She's attractive.

FLORA: In an obvious kind of way.

RICHARD: I have nothing against the obvious.

FLORA: But why her, Richard, and why now?

RICHARD: Why not?

FLORA: I think you feel humiliated.

RICHARD: What do you mean humiliated? By who?

FLORA: Her father.

RICHARD: He likes me.

FLORA: He uses you.

RICHARD: What are you talking about?

FLORA: You keep doing what he asks.

RICHARD: He's my boss.

FLORA: The quarterly statements are a joke. How can you sign them like that? I'd be angry, too. I am angry.

RICHARD: You helped me prepare them, Flora.

FLORA: Because you asked me to.

RICHARD: His strategy works. Look at the share values. This is how an economy grows.

FLORA: You can walk away from this. You're respected. Don't let him take away what's most valuable.

RICHARD: My integrity?

FLORA: Yes.

RICHARD: What I'm doing is more aggressive, but not wrong.

FLORA: You're caught in his momentum. You're doing things you don't want to do.

RICHARD: I'm learning to innovate, to think outside the box.

FLORA: Did Ben invite you to go sailing with her? Did he? He knew you'd be attracted. He's got you coming and going and you can't see it. You're blind.

RICHARD: You really don't like him, do you?

FLORA: No, nor his assistant, Paul. They are both scum.

RICHARD: Scum? You really think so?

FLORA: Yes.

RICHARD: I'm sorry to hear you say that. You aren't needed here anymore.

FLORA: Richard!

RICHARD: I have to fire you.

FLORA: You don't mean that.

RICHARD: One year's salary is the severance you'll get. A month for each year we've worked together. The check will be ready in the morning. I will miss you.

FLORA: I'm not going anywhere. I don't accept this.

RICHARD: It's not your choice. Wait more than three days before signing the release and I'll offer you nothing. I'll find cause.

FLORA: I'll find a lawyer.

RICHARD: Find a very good lawyer, an expensive lawyer, one who will cost you all your savings to come to the same conclusion as my lawyer, paid for by this company, that your professional training was not commensurate with the responsibilities of your new position.

FLORA: You can't do that.

RICHARD: Scum? Scum? You forced me to fire you.

FLORA: Richard!

Ben and Paul enter the office.

BEN: I came to say that I am very impressed by how you present our results. Our statements for the quarter are beyond good, they are ... beautiful. *(pause)* Perhaps I have come at an odd moment. I'm sorry. Should I leave the two of you alone?

RICHARD: No. At a good moment. Difficult, but clear. I am very sorry to say that Flora has decided she can't take the strain of my new position.

FLORA: He's right. I can't take it anymore. I can't. I didn't realize how big the change would be.

RICHARD: We have worked together a long time. It is an emotional moment.

BEN: Perhaps all you need is to take a holiday, some R & R. Richard's been down to my place on the Coast, taken the odd week-end to sail, do you want to do the same thing?

FLORA: No, thank you. That's not it.

BEN: Well, I count on Richard to take good care of you. Loyalty should be rewarded.

FLORA: You know him, he thinks of everything, no detail left for later. I apologize for my emotions. I know this office is not the right place for them.

Flora exits.

BEN: Is she burnt out?

RICHARD: It's all too much for her. Over the years she's tried hard, been accommodating, but …

BEN: Is she getting old, can't take the pace?

RICHARD: Well …

BEN: We'll find you a younger, better, assistant.

RICHARD: Thank you.

BEN: The statements are great.

RICHARD: I am only an accountant.

BEN: Just adding numbers?

RICHARD: Sometimes I choose which number to put where.

BEN: And I'm very glad you do.

RICHARD: Expenses that could be write-downs have been allocated to the start-ups. They're not in our statements.

BEN: Did you ask the auditors?

RICHARD: Of course. They think it a bit clever, but doable.

BEN: Clever but doable. I like that. I love that. But they signed off, and that's why they get the big bucks.

RICHARD: They're not too demanding.

BEN: As long as they can justify it.

RICHARD: I understand.

BEN: Richard, if you'll let me, I'd like to ask the Board to allow you to cash in some of your share options. I know that's where the real rewards lie, and I certainly don't want you to feel as if your talents aren't being recognized.

RICHARD: The timing is good.

BEN: Buy yourself a new car.

RICHARD: Is that an order?

BEN: Only if it's red, low to the ground, and has twelve cylinders. Enjoy yourself, Richard. You've earned it.

RICHARD: Maybe I'll ask Monica to help me choose it.

BEN: What do you mean?

RICHARD: She seems to know about things that go fast.

BEN: I worry about her sometimes. She can be so cynical.

RICHARD: Cynicism doesn't help.

BEN: No, it doesn't. I wish she had better friends, people who would respect her for who she is, had a more positive outlook.

RICHARD: I wish I could help.

BEN: Perhaps you can. Be honest with her. Point her in the right direction. Let her know you respect her. I think you're doing great work. The statements will melt in the investors' mouths like ice cream. Congratulations.

SCENE TEN

An outdoor barbecue at Holly and Ben's. It is dusk, and during the scene artificial lights replace the light of the weakening sun. Lera and Monica are arriving together.

LERA: I feel like a fraud being here.

MONICA: This is the America everyone dreams of. Relax and enjoy it. It's the good life.

LERA: It may be what everybody wants but I don't belong.

Holly can be seen approaching to greet them.

MONICA: Give them a chance. Just let the strangeness wash over you. Mother, this is Lera. I told you about her.

HOLLY: Lera, how nice to meet you. Monica, you look wonderful.

MONICA: Thank you, Mother. You don't always think so. Is there a place to get a tall drink?

HOLLY: There's a bar just over there, sweetie. Would you like something, Lera?

LERA: Do you have cold vodka?

MONICA: I'll find it. The usual, mother?

Monica exits

HOLLY: She told me you are a fabulous dancer.

LERA: She's exaggerating.

HOLLY: She said you studied ballet in Russia.

LERA: I started when I was four years old.

HOLLY:	Moscow?
LERA:	No. I've never lived in Moscow.
HOLLY:	St. Petersburg?
LERA:	To dance in St. Petersburg! No. That was just a dream.
HOLLY:	Dreams come true.
LERA:	I'm from Novokuznetsk.
HOLLY:	Where is that?
LERA:	Siberia.
HOLLY:	Siberia? Is that where the prisoners were sent?
LERA:	Yes.
HOLLY:	We Americans have always loved Russian dancers. There was Baryshnikov, and before him there was … what's his name, died of AIDS?
LERA:	Nureyev.
HOLLY:	Yes, Nureyev. The legs on the man. Like tree trunks. Which company do you dance with here?
LERA:	I don't dance anymore.
HOLLY:	Why not? You're still so young.
LERA:	I have a child who needs my time.
HOLLY:	Monica didn't tell me that. Cling to these precious years. Children are wonderful, especially when they're little.

Monica brings three drinks.

LERA:	Thank you.

Ben enters with Ivan.

BEN: What are you talking about, the wall came down, communism died, we beat you.

IVAN: You didn't beat us. A bad system collapsed.

BEN: It was Reagan and Star Wars who beat you. You knew you couldn't win, so you folded, like a gambler with a bad hand and no cash.

IVAN: Why can't you give us credit for how we rid ourselves of a totalitarian government?

BEN: Is the truth that hard for you to swallow?

IVAN: Your truth isn't true.

BEN: Has anyone seen Richard? He's supposed to be here.

MONICA: He must be here, I just parked behind his new car.

BEN: A new car? Good for him!

IVAN: It's not as if we were asleep and the American came and kissed us and we woke up.

BEN: What the fuck are you talking about? Does anyone know what the fuck he is talking about? Snow White? I was talking history and he's talking Snow White.

HOLLY: I think the reference is to Sleeping Beauty.

MONICA: It must be his car. He asked me what I would buy and I told him, and now it's parked in front of our house.

BEN: In front?

IVAN: Russians have never been defeated in a war.

MONICA: The black Porsche, with the top down.

Ben leads Ivan go to look at the car.

BEN: Yes you were, by the Japanese, in 1905.

IVAN: Aside from that.

BEN: I have to be honest with you, Ivan, your naiveté
            surprises me. It really does. What the hell are they
            teaching you over there?

HOLLY: Boys and their toys.

MONICA: How's your drink, mother?

HOLLY: It's very nice.

Richard enters from the other side.

LERA: Who is that man over there?

MONICA: That's the Richard no-one can find. Excuse me a
            minute.

She leaves to speak to Richard.

LERA: Do you mind if I stay with you?

HOLLY: I would appreciate it if someone stayed with me.

Monica meets up with Richard.

RICHARD: You look very pretty.

MONICA: Everything I suggested, down to the leather in
            olive green. It's beautiful.

RICHARD: You can drive it whenever you want.

MONICA: Why didn't you call me?

RICHARD: I've been busy.

MONICA:	Doing what?
RICHARD:	It's been frenetic at work, and in the middle of it I had to fire my executive assistant. She started to tell me her fantasies, naked people crawling towards her on their knees. I think it excited her.
MONICA:	She didn't really say that.
RICHARD:	The tension gets to people. They get weird thoughts, even the assistants.
MONICA:	Maybe she was happy you let her go.
RICHARD:	She didn't seem too happy.
MONICA:	What will she do?
RICHARD:	Do? She'll do nothing. She's not like you. She's not a fighter.
MONICA:	You think of me as a fighter?
RICHARD:	Aren't you?
MONICA:	What am I fighting for?
RICHARD:	I don't know. What are you fighting for?
MONICA:	Your attention.
RICHARD:	You have my undivided attention.
MONICA:	As a woman, not as the daughter to your boss.
RICHARD:	Your father thinks you don't have the right friends.
MONICA:	Did he tell you to tell me that?
RICHARD:	He wants me to be honest with you.
MONICA:	And you oblige?

RICHARD: Of course. I want to be honest, so that when we do the inevitable you will know that I have broken his trust, and you will know that I am not a nice man, and in spite of that, maybe because of that, you will still want me.

MONICA: I want you now. *(Pause)* It doesn't have to take long.

Monica and Richard exit while Holly and Lera continue their conversation.

LERA: She said whoever knows the present sees the future.

HOLLY: A soothsayer in Freeport. Well, why not?

LERA: Ivan said she was just crazy.

HOLLY: There's a difference between crazy stupid and crazy smart.

LERA: In Russia we respect holy fools.

HOLLY: I like that expression, Holy Fool. That's what my husband would call me, if he ever thought about it.

Ben and Ivan are approaching.

BEN: Are you going to deny that, too, Ivan, that it's the greatest country in the history of the world?

IVAN: No one denies that it is the most powerful.

BEN: You can't say it, can you? It just won't come out, the greatest country in the history of the world. The car is there, but not Richard.

HOLLY: We found him. Well, Monica found him. I don't know where they went.

BEN: They disappeared together?

HOLLY: Is my husband telling you that America has merged Roman power with Greek ideals, a world empire based on democratic principles?

IVAN: Something like that.

BEN: It's amazing but true. An extraordinary time.

IVAN: You see no contradiction between empire and democracy?

BEN: That's the problem with you Europeans, you look for intellectual contradictions, not at reality, not at the facts. A world empire based on democratic principles.

IVAN: The only people who believe that speak English.

LERA: I found God, here, in the United States.

HOLLY: That's a wonderful thing to hear you say.

LERA: I prayed for a miracle, I prayed heart and soul. And it happened. It happened here.

IVAN: Superstition runs deep in the Russian soul.

LERA: Don't you believe me?

BEN: Did you know I studied the Greeks in university? Of course you didn't know, anyhow, it interested me, I had a certain passion for it, but I confess I don't think studying their books brings us closer to them. Not really. You know when we get close, when we're outside, the sun is falling and we smell smoke and roasting meat. Incredible. This moment, when it begins to get dark and the charcoal pit is red-hot, the fat drips, flares, and the spits are turning.

HOLLY: Like the Greek army feasting on the beach at Troy.

BEN: That's it exactly.

HOLLY: After a gruelling day of golf.

BEN: You don't think the Greeks played games? Christ,
           how do you think the Olympics got started?

HOLLY: My husband is an elder in a Christian Church,
           but he much prefers to think of himself as a Greek
           Stoic.

BEN: Don't knock the Stoics. *(Ben's cell phone rings. He
           answers it.)* Ben here. Yeah, yeah. *(He puts his hand
           over the mouth.)* I have to take this.

Ben steps away

HOLLY: Stoicism also has something to do with suffering
           in silence. You know, you cut yourself, you don't
           let anybody know. Ben suffers, but he'd be damned
           before he admitted it.

IVAN: He suffers?

LERA: Ivan, why don't you believe me? What happened
           on the beach, don't you think that was a miracle?

IVAN: There isn't a God who listens to your prayers.

HOLLY: But it's a beautiful idea for a God, isn't it?

IVAN: Yes, but it's just an idea, a thought.

HOLLY: We experience life through ideas and thoughts,
           why shouldn't we experience God the same way?

IVAN: Those thoughts are just wishes.

HOLLY: I agree. Religions *are* wishes. The deepest wishes
           we have. Tell me your deepest desire and I'll tell
           you your religion. *(She sees Monica and Richard
           approaching.)* The prodigal child returns.

MONICA: I was showing Richard through the greenhouse.

HOLLY:	It's quite beautiful in there, isn't it?
RICHARD:	Yes, it is.
HOLLY:	Are there still blossoms?
MONICA:	Yes.
HOLLY:	You seem a bit distracted.
MONICA:	Do I?
HOLLY:	Lera was telling me she prayed heart and soul and that her prayers were answered. Here, in America.
MONICA:	Did she tell you why she had to pray?
HOLLY:	No, but I'm sure it's personal.
RICHARD:	Where's Ben?
HOLLY:	He was looking for you.
LERA:	Don't do that to me, Monica.
MONICA:	You're only telling her part of the story.
LERA:	Your mother understands. She's a holy fool.
MONICA:	My mother is a lovely woman who drinks too much. She doesn't understand a thing about you.

Ben is finishing his call. Richard approaches him.

BEN:	Where were you?
RICHARD:	You asked me to talk to your daughter, so I took the opportunity for a frank exchange.
BEN:	You talked to her? Well, how did it go?
RICHARD:	I thought it went well. She appreciated my concern.
BEN:	She didn't think you were being intrusive?

RICHARD: No. It was fine. Surprisingly direct.

BEN: She's a bit like me that way.

RICHARD: You must be proud of her.

BEN: Paul just called. He can't make it tonight.

RICHARD: I sometimes wonder about him, his loyalty.

BEN: Do you? Why?

RICHARD: I don't think you should pay attention to
           my intuitions.

BEN: It's my job to pay attention. You are new in a tough
           position and you've brought a lot of good insight
           into the corporation. Believe me, I pay attention
           to your intuitions.

RICHARD: Thank you. Coming from you that means something.

BEN: Everybody! Listen up! Let's make our way to the
           spits. I want to show you how our chef carves. It's
           an art form, how to separate meat from the bone,
           an ancient art form largely lost. But I found a man
           who knows how to do it. It is a wonder to watch.
           Perfect steaks fall from the animal.

ACT TWO

SCENE ELEVEN

Flora has asked for, and received, a meeting with Paul.

PAUL: So, how can I help you? If you want a reference or employment advice there are people better than I.

FLORA: I confess I never liked you, Paul.

PAUL: Do you always start with a compliment?

FLORA: But I am capable of changing my opinion.

PAUL: How magnanimous of you! Look, Flora, I'm busy. I understand that you took the check and signed the severance papers.

FLORA: I did.

PAUL: So why this meeting?

FLORA: You know that Richard is paying himself from the capital resources of the start-ups.

PAUL: I do. Professional fees for professional services.

FLORA: He's getting paid by three different start-ups as well as the mother company.

PAUL: You have a point?

FLORA: A touch odd.

PAUL: Our accountants believe it to be justified.

FLORA: As if they care!

PAUL: Have I missed something? Are you an expert? I mean, what right do you have to question the largest and most respected accounting firm in the world? They have forensic accountants who pour over our books on a regular basis in incredible detail and you, if I have this right, an executive assistant, a secretary if we cut the crap, believes she has the background and knowledge to question them?

FLORA: I know when certain things aren't normal practice.

PAUL: You do?

FLORA: I know when major expenses either don't show up or are being wrongly recorded as equity investments. I know false projections when I see them.

PAUL: Those are serious allegations.

FLORA: Our clients won't pay that kind of mark-up.

PAUL: Energy requirements are up, a grid can only handle so much:—distribution choices have to be made.

FLORA: That's blackmail.

PAUL: It's hard to argue when the lights are out.

FLORA: There is no shortage!

PAUL: We sincerely regret the rolling blackouts, but it's important to us that no region bear more of a burden than another.

FLORA: I need to speak to Ben directly.

PAUL: These are critical days in the energy sector. The President can't meet with every incompetent secretary who gets fired. Just tell me what you want.

FLORA: I want my self-respect back.

PAUL: Maybe its not self-respect you're after.

FLORA:	What do you mean?
PAUL:	You want to see Richard hurt, don't you, and for him to know that it's you who hurt him. Yes? Yes? Go on, you can be honest. Is that what you want?
FLORA:	Yes.
PAUL:	How long did you work with Richard?
FLORA:	Twelve years.
PAUL:	Did you do a lot of the work during that time?
FLORA:	Especially on the statements.
PAUL:	I'm sorry if you've been treated unfairly.
FLORA:	I don't want your compassion.
PAUL:	It's the best I can do.
FLORA:	I want to see a mutual enemy destroyed.
PAUL:	Why do you think he's a mutual enemy?
FLORA:	Ben trusts him more than you. You know that.
PAUL:	We could get together tomorrow night.
FLORA:	We need a plan.
PAUL:	No. Just time to talk.
FLORA:	A fresh start? I'll buy a new dress.
PAUL:	You want to make this easy for me.
FLORA:	I am trying, Paul. Do you have a favorite color?
PAUL:	I'm a prairie boy, did you know that? When I was a kid I used to watch the wind ripple the wheat. And I remember, on hot days, walking through that pale golden world. The color, the smell, the heat.
FLORA:	Yellow. I would never have expected that.

PAUL: I would like it if everything you wore were pale yellow.

FLORA: Everything?

PAUL: How do I know I'm not being set up? How do I know you're not still loyal to Richard, and that you won't come in wired, and record everything?

FLORA: I hadn't even thought of that.

PAUL: Why enter this world, Flora? This is a good country if you don't ask too many questions. Think about it. Just take the money and run.

FLORA: Everything I wear will be pale yellow. I won't be wired for sound. You can check. I expect you to be slow and thorough.

SCENE TWELVE

Nora and Lera are on the beach.

NORA: Shreds of seaweed, small broken shells, a plastic lid for a coffee cup, the tracks of a car, traces of crabs who have dragged themselves along the moist sand, an empty claw! Look.

LERA: The water is still.

NORA: Won't last.

LERA: No.

NORA: Sometimes I look at this beach during a terrible storm and I see peace and harmony. Sometimes I walk along on a calm day like today and see violence and change. The evidence for both is always here.

LERA:	This beach means a lot to me.
NORA:	Think of all the living creatures that have visited it, not just today, but over the years, over the ages. It comforts me to think of that.
LERA:	Comforts you?
NORA:	Yes.
LERA:	You can see them?
NORA:	In my mind's eye. Sometimes I even imagine extinct animals here on the beach.
LERA:	Can one see through time like that?
NORA:	No, not really.
LERA:	I thought you would say that we could. I mean, I came here so that you would tell me my future.
NORA:	I know.
LERA:	Well?
NORA:	I just try to see the present, the only revelation I trust.
LERA:	I'm sick.
NORA:	I'm sorry.
LERA:	They say there is no cure. I don't want to die.
NORA:	I understand.
LERA:	I have my child, she is so young. Who will take care of her?
NORA:	You have to decide that.
LERA:	I feel weaker all the time. I'm not winning. I've been fighting so hard and I'm not winning.

NORA: I had an image when I held your hands. I saw you flying on the back of a moth.

LERA: A moth?

NORA: With white wings. You were twisting, turning, almost dancing, and then night. Well, not night, black water.

LERA: What will happen to my child?

NORA: I don't know.

LERA: Who will take care of her?

NORA: Choose someone and ask them.

LERA: I am angry. I'm so angry. These tears are anger.

NORA: You must know someone who needs the love of a child.

LERA: No.

NORA: Someone.

LERA: No.

NORA: For the child's sake.

LERA: Maybe.

NORA: Ask her.

SCENE THIRTEEN

Paul enters with Ben

PAUL: I met with Richard's fired assistant.

BEN: Fired? He didn't fire her. She quit. I was there. Something about not wanting the strain anymore.

PAUL:	That's not how she remembers it.
BEN:	That's how I remember it.
PAUL:	She wants to tell you about Richard's sins.
BEN:	I don't want to listen.
PAUL:	She has a good idea of where the statements reflect usual practice and where they are … optimistic.
BEN:	What does she want?
PAUL:	She hopes you will be morally outraged and force Richard to resign in disgrace.
BEN:	Is she that simple?
PAUL:	It's not about intelligence. It's about the shape of her moral universe.
BEN:	I see.
PAUL:	She has a list of documents that were shredded. She wants to take it to the Securities Commissioner.
BEN:	So? What would he do with it? He has the job because he hasn't a tooth in his mouth. Probably owns our shares.
PAUL:	Then again, she might go to the media. They always love the underdog whistle blower. She'll cry to the cameras that she was fired for telling the truth. She'll perform admirably.
BEN:	It's pretty obvious that she's playing you.
PAUL:	She also said that Richard and I are enemies and that you are on his side.
BEN:	You want to go up against me, Paul?
PAUL:	No. I just want the truth.

BEN: He asked if I trusted you, as if I shouldn't.

PAUL: He's feeling cocky.

BEN: He wants Monica. Something is going on.

PAUL: She's an attractive girl, she has options. Why would she go with him?

BEN: Maybe because she's had everyone else.

PAUL: Do you want to talk about this?

BEN: No.

PAUL: All right.

BEN: Has she fucked you yet, Paul? She prefers to do it with the people I work with.

PAUL: You know, the only investors buying now are the foreign mutuals and the little guys. The smart money knows the bubble can't last.

BEN: Trying to change the subject?

PAUL: The original money is out, ten times over.

BEN: Not too shabby.

PAUL: We call in the Exchange Commission ourselves, express concerns with the statements, missing documents, misleading numbers, errors. They agree to bring charges against Richard for fraud, make it front page news, handcuffs, photos, the works. It will look good for the Commissioner, as if he's alive, and we can show, you, I, the Board, that we acted with extreme urgency as soon as we knew what was going on.

BEN: There'll be a lot of noise. A lot of anger.

PAUL:	Flora gives us deniability. We never knew. And that's the point, as soon as she talked, we acted. If they believe her, then they'll have to believe us.
BEN:	Will they believe her?
PAUL:	She talks from her heart. She'll be perfect.
BEN:	Let's do it. Time is now.

SCENE FOURTEEN

Lera is with Monica.

MONICA:	You can't ask me to do that.
LERA:	Why not?
MONICA:	You know what I'm like.
LERA:	I trust you.
MONICA:	I don't do anything right. I hate responsibility. I am attracted to the wrong men for the wrong reason. I've had abortions of my own.
LERA:	You're smart, you're brave. You're honest, open. You know me. You know her. She likes you.
MONICA:	I don't have what it takes. I'm sorry. I wish I were the right person. I do. I think your daughter is great, but—
LERA:	Don't say 'but'.
MONICA:	She deserves better.
LERA:	I'll judge that.
MONICA:	Why are you talking like this? You look good.
LERA:	Get real, Monica.

MONICA:	Do you really think I can do it?
LERA:	I can't think of anybody better.

SCENE FIFTEEN

Paul enters with Richard

PAUL:	Ben wants to deal with the crisis quickly, forthrightly.
RICHARD:	What crisis?
PAUL:	We can make the best of a bad situation: write down some of the more dubious investments, cut payroll, set new targets.
RICHARD:	What situation?
PAUL:	You know, it never looks good when executives cash in stock options prior to a profit warning, even those with squeaky clean reputations. It looks like insider trading.
RICHARD:	Who's talking about a profit warning?
PAUL:	Ben is.
RICHARD:	I don't understand.
PAUL:	He wants to make sure we have clean statements, all revenues conservative, all expenses known.
RICHARD:	Jesus! Why now?
PAUL:	What do you mean why now?
RICHARD:	I don't understand.
PAUL:	What don't you understand?
RICHARD:	Have I lost Ben's confidence?

PAUL: It's your job to protect the shareholders' interests
           with the utmost integrity. Ben has to ask himself if
           you're delivering that.

RICHARD: Why are we changing strategies?

PAUL: We're not changing strategies.

RICHARD: We could have had a profit warning for every
           quarter I've been here. So, Paul, why the hell now?

PAUL: You are perceiving this in the worst possible way.

RICHARD: This is not about my fucking perceptions! Why has
           nobody talked to me?

PAUL: I'm talking to you now. And I'm telling you that
           we've never wanted to mislead the public!

RICHARD: We can't come clean from one statement to the
           next! We'll create panic! It will be a disaster!

PAUL: Come clean? You admit to falsifying documents?

RICHARD: Am I being set up?

PAUL: Why are you talking like that?

RICHARD: I want this conversation with Ben, not you.

PAUL: Ben has a list of documents that were shredded by
           you. It didn't make him happy when he read it.

RICHARD: I never shredded documents!

PAUL: You gave the orders.

RICHARD: What evidence is there for that? Find me one scrap
           of evidence!

PAUL: Funny thing, once a jury knows that documents
           have been destroyed, they don't need written
           evidence. They're not stupid. All they're going to
           need is Flora on the stand.

RICHARD:	Flora, on the stand?
PAUL:	She gave us the list.
RICHARD:	What do you mean, on the stand?
PAUL:	As in 'give evidence'.
RICHARD:	At a trial?
PAUL:	Not too fast today, are we?
RICHARD:	She won't take the stand. I know her. We worked together for twelve years. The problem with you is that you know sweet fuck all about loyalty. Flora does. She isn't scum like you. That's what she called you. Scum.
PAUL:	You fired her for telling you the truth about the statements.
RICHARD:	I didn't fire her. She quit.
PAUL:	She doesn't remember it that way.
RICHARD:	You're setting up the wrong man, Paul.
PAUL:	She's easy to believe, has nothing to lose, was wronged by a rich aggressive male with low ethical standards.
RICHARD:	Go fuck yourself!
PAUL:	You can react in anger, be indicted and jailed, or you can work with us, confess the crimes, and maybe we can get you off with just a fine. It's that simple, Richard, those are the choices.
RICHARD:	I'm the bad guy? I'm the criminal? Me?
PAUL:	And you're going to get nailed!
RICHARD:	I don't think so.

PAUL: Don't bother going back to your office. The lock's being changed. Your computer and back-up discs are being held as evidence. Your personal effects will be delivered to you. Can you find your way to the exit, or would you prefer I call an escort?

SCENE SIXTEEN

Monica is talking to Ivan

MONICA: Someone has to talk to her in Russian, help her with a sense of who she is, where she's from.

IVAN: I don't know how long I'll be here. When they tell me to go back I will.

MONICA: So? You can talk on the phone, or email her. When she gets older she can visit you in Moscow or St. Petersburg. Maybe you could take her to Novokuznetsk, show her where her mother was born.

IVAN: I've never been there myself.

MONICA: But you know it exists.

IVAN: She has no family?

MONICA: No.

IVAN: No boyfriend?

MONICA: She doesn't like men, Ivan. She's not like me that way. But she felt something for you. Perhaps because you're from home, because you're young and naive.

IVAN: I'm not naive.

MONICA: Yes you are.

IVAN:	Why do you think that?
MONICA:	You're an intellectual.
IVAN:	You resent me because I think.
MONICA:	Everybody thinks, it's just that, being an intellectual, you have a hard time grasping that.
IVAN:	Give me a break.
MONICA:	Do you know how Lera came to America? She didn't just ring the front doorbell and get invited in.
IVAN:	I asked.
MONICA:	The ad in a local paper said opportunities for girls to dance in Paradise. That's what it said.
IVAN:	Those ads are in the papers all the time. We laugh at them. How could anyone be so stupid to believe it?
MONICA:	Three answered from her town. Lera was sixteen, the two others were even younger: a train to Odessa; then on a tanker in a hold without windows. They never saw the sky, never saw the water. Night before they landed they were forced to fuck the crew. They thought the worst was over. Thought they'd dance in a bar and quit to find something better, but were driven to a locked house where they joined six other girls. Siberians pride themselves on being tough, but humans have limits. One drank a bottle of bleach, the other broke a window and slashed her tits and back trying to slide out.
IVAN:	I don't want to hear this.
MONICA:	Lera took the drugs. If you take the drugs you don't fight. Don't fight you don't get beaten. She took drugs and lay there, and became pregnant. They

organized an abortion. Lera didn't mind, not like she was trying to start a family. Christ. They had to take a sample of her blood to the doctor. He told them that she had HIV. So they didn't want her anymore – drove her to the middle of the city – let her go. That was when she learned she was in Houston. Five months later she had her baby on the beach.

IVAN: She told me about that.

MONICA: She insists it's not a sad story. Strange, isn't it? It was HIV saved her baby's life.

IVAN: Does her child have it?

MONICA: She thinks that's the miracle. She prayed over and over for the baby to be okay, and she was. The doctors say about half of infected mothers pass it along. A fifty-fifty chance.

IVAN: I don't know if I can do it.

MONICA: You're not talking to her, you're talking to me. You can say no.

SCENE SEVENTEEN

Richard and Monica

RICHARD: Your father set me up.

MONICA: Principles aren't his strong suit.

RICHARD: You can say that about your father?

MONICA: He likes it when I talk trash about him. Makes him feel that I'm realistic.

RICHARD: I thought my eyes were open.

MONICA: Said the blind man.

RICHARD: Do you love me?

MONICA: I have feelings.

RICHARD: Come here. Kiss me gently.

They kiss gently.

MONICA: I'm going to New York this week-end.

RICHARD: What's in New York you can't buy here?

MONICA: Time with my parents.

RICHARD: Kiss me again.

They kiss passionately

MONICA: What's gotten into you? Are you becoming romantic?

RICHARD: Would you like that?

MONICA: It would be different. Might be nice. Have a regular relationship. Take care of a child.

RICHARD: I want to be held and I want to tear someone's heart out.

MONICA: It's okay, Richard. Don't stress.

RICHARD: I don't know who I am. When I talk I can't hear my own voice. I hear someone else.

MONICA: We can get through this. We can. I'll only be gone for the weekend.

SCENE EIGHTEEN

Richard is meeting with Mike

RICHARD: What do I call you?

MIKE: Do I need a name?

RICHARD: Can I call you The Man?

MIKE: If you want.

RICHARD: No defining characteristics?

MIKE: I like movies. Is that specific enough?

RICHARD: Regular guy.

MIKE: I have friends with a method.

RICHARD: What is that method?

MIKE: It changes. It can't be defined. It's invisible. Maybe a car accident. Maybe bad food. Maybe a heart attack. Stairs. I never know, and you'll never know either and really, it's better that way.

RICHARD: The payment?

MIKE: All cash upfront.

RICHARD: I can't agree to that.

MIKE: I never said it was negotiable.

RICHARD: They could just walk away with the money.

MIKE: They could, but they won't.

RICHARD: You're asking me to trust you?

MIKE: This isn't a trust thing. It's not a dating service where everybody tries to like everyone. This is different. It's an organized ignorance kind of thing. The guys who do this will never meet you, you won't meet them, and this meeting never happened. I don't know your name, you don't need mine. All I need from you, right now, is the name and address of the target. Write it on this piece of paper and put it in this envelope. Seal it. Very good. I'll never know what you wrote. You might have written Daffy Duck for all I know. That's it. That's all. Clean.

RICHARD: I want it to happen quickly.

MIKE: Why do you tell me that? That makes no sense. It's not in your wishes, it's not in my hands. We're not involved.

SCENE NINETEEN

Monica joins Holly on the plane.

HOLLY: Your father is supposed to be with you.

MONICA: He can't make it.

HOLLY: Isn't that a surprise. Oh well, you are more fun to shop with.

MONICA: That wouldn't be too hard.

HOLLY: Your father has his virtues.

MONICA: He's shafting Richard.

HOLLY: Do you know the whole story?

MONICA: No.

HOLLY: How is your accountant?

MONICA: He's being investigated by the feds.

HOLLY:	I meant within the relationship.
MONICA:	Showing signs of becoming romantic.
HOLLY:	A romantic accountant? Isn't that an oxymoron? *(the plane starts down the runway)* Oh God, why do I always hate this part? I just close my eyes and hope that everything works.
MONICA:	You're so silly.
HOLLY:	I know.
MONICA:	Is that better?
HOLLY:	Yes, as soon as we get a bit more height I'll lose all fear and it will be smooth sailing.
MONICA:	There's something I want to talk to you about. I've made a decision.
HOLLY:	I'm listening.
MONICA:	I've decided to parent a child.
HOLLY:	Are you pregnant?
MONICA:	It's Lera's child.
HOLLY:	Who's Lera?
MONICA:	You met her at the barbecue. The dancer.
HOLLY:	A very nice girl. A real dancer's body.
MONICA:	She has AIDS.
HOLLY:	Oh, I'm sorry. I really am.
MONICA:	I promised her, when she can't do it herself, or when she dies, to take care of her child.
HOLLY:	Are you ready for that?
MONICA:	She asked me.

HOLLY:	It's hard work.
MONICA:	You think I shouldn't do it?
HOLLY:	Don't be defensive. I liked Lera very much. But you have to admit that you are used to being selfish, to living for yourself. A child is a lifetime of responsibility.
MONICA:	All my life I've been given everything and been told I was too selfish. All my life you and Dad have wanted me to get more and complained that I had too much.
HOLLY:	I'm sorry.
MONICA:	I want to take care of someone else's child and your first reaction is to say that I'm too selfish.
HOLLY:	I shouldn't have said that.
MONICA:	Or do you think I'm being taken advantage of by some diseased foreigner?
HOLLY:	That never occurred to me. Do you think that?
MONICA:	No! No, I feel honored. I feel like, like … I don't want to say reborn but …
HOLLY:	… and you want me to help you?
MONICA:	You know, when a woman has a child her mother comes and helps …
HOLLY:	She's the grandmother after all.
MONICA:	That's right. Exactly right.
HOLLY:	If you put your mind to it, I'm sure you'll be great.
MONICA:	You haven't said that to me for a while. But I am not great, am I, in spite of all the times I've put my mind to it? I mean, I'm fit, physically fit, ridiculously so, but …

HOLLY: You're being hard on yourself.

MONICA: Maybe it's me, Mother. Maybe I need to say it out
            loud and really hear myself saying it. Maybe it's me.
            But I can change. Tell me I can change, tell me that.

*There is a muffled boom on the plane, and Holly and Monica begin
to fall, strapped into their seats.*

HOLLY: I am thinking of my child's emotional pain, and
            I am wondering how I can help her through her
            dark thoughts and new situation when I hear a
            muffled boom. The plane slips to the side and rolls
            and rolls again and begins to dive, and I know
            with a certainty that I will die. Adrenaline is racing
            through me and I am intensely aware of being
            frightened. But I am not frightened of pain, I am
            frightened of annihilation. I turn to say something
            to my child beside me. I know that she will die. My
            child is going to die beside me strapped into that
            chair, annihilated, and I don't … There is horror
            on my baby's face, how can anyone die like that
            with such fear it is wrong that this moment should
            be her last, I am yelling something at her, to her,
            telling her that I am with her but she can't hear me,
            she can't, but now she is turning and looking in my
            eyes my dear baby who I love and we are spiralling
            down … do not let her die do not let her die do not
            let her die … down, down, falling, the whine is so
            loud but suddenly the world has slowed to a crawl,
            infinitesimally slow movements, and I realize that
            if there is compassion in the world, woven into the
            very fabric of the universe then … a silent prayer
            of grace of thanks of love in my heart fills my chest

runs through my arm into my hand clinging now
merged as one with the hand of Monica I love you
who needs me I send you this silent prayer … we
are not being annihilated we are entering …

SCENE TWENTY

Nora is alone on the beach. She speaks directly to the audience.

NORA: I saw a small jet dive into the Gulf. It was gaining
elevation, turning in a sweeping arc as if to head
north and east. Then it seemed to slip, as if surfing
an invisible tide, before spinning, tilting, now
diving towards the water, the blue water reflecting
an untroubled sky. I thought it might be a great
hungry bird which had spotted a remarkable fish
below the surface, and whined in expectation, and
broke into a piercing exultant cry when closer,
then disappeared with a great splash, an explosion
of water followed by an impenetrable silence. I half
expected to see the plane burst out of the water,
as if it really had been a bird sweeping down and
hunting within the cool depths, and that it would
rise with the flashing of a large silver fish in its
mouth, but the water calmed. In no time, not even
five minutes, the waves had taken on their usual
rhythm. It was astonishingly peaceful. The color of
the sky had not changed. The few clouds had not
moved. And yet this terrible, appalling violence
had just happened. In front of my eyes. Not far
away. Just there.

SCENE TWENTY-ONE

Richard approaches Ben, who is leaving a memorial service for Monica and Holly.

RICHARD: I want to give you my condolences.

BEN: Were you here for the memorial service?

RICHARD: I had to come. In spite of everything.

BEN: That's kind of you.

RICHARD: It's very hard to understand.

BEN: Mechanical. The engine.

RICHARD: That's what they say.

BEN: You had met my wife, hadn't you? Yes, with Monica, that first night. Long ago.

RICHARD: I met her several times.

BEN: Monica talked about goldfish. Something about measuring their memories. Two seconds, she said.

RICHARD: That's right.

BEN: It was funny, wasn't it? 'Look, a castle'. I laughed. I will never forget them. Never. Not ever.

RICHARD: I'm sorry.

BEN: You know, I was supposed to be on that plane.

RICHARD: I didn't know that.

BEN: I would gladly have given my life for theirs.

RICHARD: I understand.

BEN: Why did God save me? Why?

RICHARD: I don't know.

BEN: Maybe he didn't want me to die with the soul I had. Maybe he was offering me a chance to change.

RICHARD: To change?

BEN: Holly believed in a loving god.

RICHARD: You think they are in heaven?

BEN: Maybe not the heaven you imagine, but yes, their souls will find peace.

RICHARD: Eternal peace.

BEN: Are you making fun of me?

RICHARD: No.

BEN: I don't expect you to believe me.

RICHARD: Are you calling their death a blessing?

BEN: What matters is not why you find God, but that God is there to be found. I have faith.

RICHARD: Faith?

BEN: Without faith we are only clay, no, not clay, shit. Shit! The stuff that stinks on the bottom of your shoe. But with faith, we are saved.

RICHARD: You have a soul?

BEN: You don't?

RICHARD: I'm sure that if you have one, I do, too.

BEN: What do you want from me?

RICHARD: I want your protection from the investigators.

BEN: Ask for God's forgiveness.

RICHARD: It's your protection I want. In return, I'll help you.

BEN:	How can you help me?
RICHARD:	The name of the person who wanted your death and killed your wife and child. Do you want that?
BEN:	Maybe it was you.
RICHARD:	Would I be here if it was?
BEN:	My daughter believed in you.
RICHARD:	Trust her instincts.
BEN:	You have reason to hate me.
RICHARD:	There are many who hate you.
BEN:	Yes.
RICHARD:	Does that bother you?
BEN:	Yes.
RICHARD:	It shouldn't.
BEN:	No?
RICHARD:	They hate you because you're free. Free men make decisions. They fight for their interests. They get what they want. So they're hated.
BEN:	Do you think I've done nothing wrong?
RICHARD:	Someone wanted to kill you. Someone killed your loved ones. Justice demands revenge. Do you want to work with me on this? Do we have a deal?

SCENE TWENTY-TWO

Mike and Lera at the entrance to the Club

MIKE: Maybe you shouldn't dance tonight.

LERA: Let me change.

MIKE: I can't let you dance looking like that.

LERA: No-one can see in there.

MIKE: Maybe you have a bug or something.

LERA: I know I don't look good right now, but I'll put on make-up, fix my hair.

MIKE: I don't think that's it. I'll call you.

LERA: No, you won't.

MIKE: Nothing personal.

LERA: Just like that?

MIKE: The customers deserve better.

LERA: I'm stressed, that's all.

MIKE: Stress?

LERA: My child's mother just died.

MIKE: How can someone else be your child's mother?

LERA: Monica. She … never mind. Just go fuck yourself, Mike.

she goes to leave

MIKE: Lera, wait a second.

LERA: What?

MIKE:	The plane. Do you think it just fell out of the sky? Do you really think it was, what, an accident?
LERA:	What are you saying?
MIKE:	I liked Monica very much. She was a good girl.
LERA:	So?
MIKE:	Come here a minute.

SCENE TWENTY-THREE

Lera and Richard are sailing at night. They speak over a gathering wind.

RICHARD:	Have you ever sailed at night?
LERA:	No.
RICHARD:	It's beautiful.
LERA:	Yes. Should we have turned back earlier?
RICHARD:	Why? It was a sunny day, and now it's a clear night.
LERA:	A new moon.
RICHARD:	Almost. Not quite.
LERA:	And a thousand thousand stars.
RICHARD:	More than that. Think of a million million.
LERA:	More than we can count.
RICHARD:	When I was a kid, a hundred was big.
LERA:	The wind is picking up.
RICHARD:	Enjoy the speed.

LERA:	The sails look like wings.
RICHARD:	What?
LERA:	Do you ever think of Monica?
RICHARD:	What? You have to yell.
LERA:	Monica! Monica!!
RICHARD:	I do. But one has to move on.
LERA:	Do you ever think of Holly?
RICHARD:	I can't hear you. Don't be frightened! The wind will just get us home faster!
LERA:	Holly! Are you frightened?
RICHARD:	No!

Monica and Holly pull themselves up into the boat. Lera can see them, Richard can't. The boat tips dangerously.

RICHARD:	Why is the boat tilting? We almost went over! Why did the boat tilt like that?
MONICA:	Don't be frightened.
LERA:	I'm not.
RICHARD:	What's happening?
MONICA:	He can't see us.
HOLLY:	The holy fool, that's what you called me.
RICHARD:	You can't move about like that!
MONICA:	He's afraid.
LERA:	I want to move. I want to dance.

Lera begins to dance on the boat.

RICHARD: Don't do that!!

HOLLY: She recognizes the time.

RICHARD: Lera! What are you doing?

Lera is dancing in the wind on the tilting boat.

LERA: Reach for me, Richard. I need you to reach for me.
Here. I am just here. Reach for my hand.

Richard reaches for Lera and she pulls him towards herself as the boat capsizes.

SCENE TWENTY-FOUR

Flora is casually reading from a public statement she and Paul are preparing.

FLORA: "We didn't know when the former CFO joined the
company the quality of character that he had. He
has deceived us and we are victims of his lies."

PAUL: That's good. I can say that.

FLORA: Did you know he drowned in the arms of a
diseased prostitute?

PAUL: People should know that.

FLORA: It can be leaked to the press.

PAUL: He was an evil man.

FLORA: Evil? We can put that here: "He has deceived
us and we are paying for his evil ways. We have
challenges in front of us. We must sell certain
divisions and close down others. We have to

cut jobs. We have to be more vigilant to assure
that this sort of thing never happens again, but I
assure you …

Paul continues reading

PAUL: —"that as the new President, we will save the
            essential core. This is a company with a mission
            and a momentum."

FLORA: That's what they want to hear. Do we invite Ben to
            the meeting?

PAUL: Don't worry about him. Yesterday's man.

SCENE TWENTY-FIVE

*Nora and Ivan on the beach. With them, at a slight distance,
is Lera's young daughter.*

IVAN: Lera asked if I would take care of her for an
            evening. I said of course. She came with her little
            knapsack, a toothbrush. Lera hugged her tightly
            and then left. She never came back. I don't know
            her legal status, I don't know if she is Russian or
            American. I guess a bit of both. Her baby-sitter
            is Spanish. She speaks a mix of all three. No-one
            knows anything about her father, except that he
            was willing to pay for sex with a teenager on drugs.
            On her mother's side she is a child of Stalin's Gulag.
            She doesn't start with much.

NORA: She's a child, not a bank account.

IVAN: Did you know she was born on this beach?

NORA: Is that true?

IVAN:	Yes.
NORA:	You have to tell her that.
IVAN:	I will. And I will tell her that it was a stranger who sucked the mucous from her nose and tied her umbilical cord with a shoelace. And I will tell her that her mother loved her, fought for her, prayed for her. Can I do this, Nora. Can I?
NORA:	One day she will stand as an adult, on this beach, and rejoice in all that is good in her life.
IVAN:	I hope so.
NORA:	Will you bring her here again?
IVAN:	Would you like that?
NORA:	That would be a blessing. A real blessing.
IVAN:	She dances you know. For no reason. Just dances.
NORA:	There are reasons. Oh, there are lots of reasons. We just don't see them as clearly as she does.

KAREENA

CAST

The play takes place in Montreal between the years 1995 and 2000, although certain scenes represent Kareena's childhood memories from Odessa, Ukraine, and her imagining of events that may have happened there.

The locations of scenes varies quickly. Scenography is meant to be suggestive and fluid. When possible, sound should be privileged.

KAREENA: In her mid-twenties, Kareena is passionate, stubborn, and quixotic. It is central to the concept of the play that she sometimes takes on her mother's distinct and different persona. These moments are simply indicated in the script by **MOTHER**. Kareena is struggling towards wholeness on terms she can understand, and she succeeds.

JAROSLAW: Two years younger than his sister, he is quick of wit and only seemingly self-assured. Jaroslaw is constantly scrambling to achieve a tentative sense of balance and self-worth upon the slippery surface of his fatalism. Not only is Kareena his only sibling, but as older sister she has fulfilled the role of mother during much of his parent-less youth.

ANTONIO: Born in Italy, but long in Canada, he is in his mid-to-late fifties and has taken early retirement. His identity as socialist and teacher has sustained him during most of his adult life, but a comfortable sensualism has replaced his earlier beliefs.

NICOLE: Slightly older than Kareena, and comfortable in the bureaucracy of the Quebec government, Nicole appreciates the excitement and idiosyncrasy Jaroslaw brings into her life. As a single mother, however, she is careful not to take steps that might derail her professional position.

PETROV: An imaginary figure who appears and disappears according to Kareena's need, Petrov is a middle aged functionary who moves easily between changing regimes. Not uncommon in the Eastern Europe of today, his biography would show someone who, in order, has been a committed communist, a nationalist, and is now a free-enterpriser.

François: In his early thirties, François is Jaroslaw's co-worker in the warehouse of a dress factory. They enjoy working together and take their breaks at the same time at Costa's tiny restaurant. They have an easy respect and mutual sympathy.

Costa: A Greek immigrant in his late fifties, Costa is the owner of a hole-in-the-wall café which gives him a meagre livelihood and the semblance of independence.

Young Kareena: Kareena at the age of six. Non-speaking.

Young Jaroslaw: Jaroslaw at the age of four. Non-speaking

Olivier: Nicole's child, can be played by same actor as Young Jaroslaw. Non-speaking

Landlord: Can be doubled with Costa

Bartender: Can be doubled with François

Bar Woman: An older woman of indeterminate age; an evocative, troubling and troubled character. It would be appropriate for the same actress to be the body double of Kareena's mother (and, therefore, the body double of Kareena herself) and be used as such at appropriate moments in the play.

Other: Small chorus of women at the funeral, people in bar, in restaurant, men on the stairs. (Appreciated, but not absolutely necessary).

The minimum cast is ten, eight actors and two non-speaking children.

SCENE ONE

A young mother wearing a simple jacket with a shawl over her head appears holding the hands of two children, a girl about six years old and a slightly younger boy. She is hurrying them towards a simple set of old and rusting swings which materialize in front of them.

We hear traffic and ambient street sounds, to which are added, faintly but distinctly, the sounds of a person breathing.

The mother can be seen leaning towards the children to talk to them. The words, in Ukrainian, telling them to play while she attends a meeting, are indistinctly woven into the texture of sounds.

The children run to the swings.

A door appears upstage of the Mother. She turns to it and enters. As she does, flights of stairs become visible behind the door, and she begins to climb them. The sound of the breathing changes to reflect the physical exertion.

At the top of the stairs another door appears, the Mother pauses, catches her breath, grabs the handle, and pulls.

SCENE TWO

Downstage, the children and swings have disappeared and elements of a small, clean apartment have taken its place.

Kareena sits up in the bathtub, and immediately the sound of breathing disappears, as if she were, all along, listening to her own breath under water.

She pulls the water from her face and her hair. She dries quickly and puts on a robe. She begins to hum a song, and soon she is softly singing the words as well.

Morning light is seeping into the apartment and around the flat white blind in Jaroslaw's room. He awakes. He listens to the melody being sung by Kareena in the next room. It is drowned out momentarily by the sound of a passing bus.

Kareena continues to sing lightly as she makes coffee and sections an orange. The kitchen is very spare except for a table and two chairs, and an oddly beautiful wooden icon which hangs on the wall behind the table.

Kareena brings a bowl of steaming coffee to Jaroslaw, who sits up in his bed. He sips the hot beverage.

JAROSLAW: It's good.

KAREENA: You always say that.

Kareena opens the blind and leaves the room. Jaroslaw rises, dresses, enters the kitchen and sits at the table. He begins to eat the orange slices.

JAROSLAW: You were up early.

KAREENA: Did I wake you?

JAROSLAW: I love it when I wake up and hear you sing. I love that.

KAREENA: Mama used to sing.

JAROSLAW: That's what you tell me.

KAREENA: I hear her voice in my head.

JAROSLAW: That's good.

KAREENA: I saw her this morning.

JAROSLAW: You saw her?

KAREENA: No, I didn't see her, I was her.

JAROSLAW: Ah, of course, you were her.

KAREENA: In the bath, before you woke, I was her. I mean I felt I was her, breathing, and then climbing stairs, entering doors.

JAROSLAW: That's nice.

KAREENA: What makes you like that? Why don't you ever think about what I tell you?

JAROSLAW: I think about things that matter.

KAREENA: I see.

JAROSLAW: Call it a dream and let it go, Kareena. Leave the moon in the sky and the knife in the drawer.

Kareena looks on in silence as Jaroslaw rapidly finishes his breakfast. He gets up to leave.

KAREENA: Are you going right away?

JAROSLAW: If I take the bus that comes now I might get a seat, otherwise I'll have to stand all the way. What are you doing today?

KAREENA: I want to go to the port, then I'll walk along the canal to the market. What would you like tonight?

JAROSLAW: You know what I like.

*Jaroslaw grabs his jacket, exits. Kareena briefly cleans up.
The sound of a bus, passing.*

Kareena puts on her jacket and the same shawl that we saw in the first scene on the Mother, but rather than wear it over her head, she wears it loosely about her shoulders.

SCENE THREE

The Old Port of Montreal. Kareena passes Antonio as she walks along the path beside the St. Lawrence river. He notices her, and speaks.

ANTONIO: Doesn't look that mighty from here, does it?

KAREENA: What?

ANTONIO: The river. The St. Lawrence. Not that mighty. Still … a beautiful river.

KAREENA: When I see it I think of the Dnipro.

ANTONIO: The what?

KAREENA: The Dnipro. It runs through Ukraine: starts in the marshes, empties in the Black Sea.

ANTONIO: I thought it was the Dneiper.

KAREENA: That's the Russian word for it. Its real name, the Ukrainian name, is the Dnipro.

ANTONIO: Its real name, of course.

KAREENA: But now, when we look at it, we think of pollution. Fish in it are born without eyes, cows who drink it have calves with eight legs. You think I'm exaggerating?

ANTONIO: No.

KAREENA: It's not just Chernobyl. The whole country has become poisoned. Perhaps that's why I'm like this.

ANTONIO: Like what?

KAREENA: What's your word, a mutant?

ANTONIO: You don't seem like a mutant to me.

KAREENA: You don't know me.

ANTONIO:	Is that why you came here, less pollution?
KAREENA:	To have a better life, to start again.
ANTONIO:	In the free world?
KAREENA:	I left Ukraine the year it became independent. But it became even poorer than before. People worked and never got paid. And when they did, the currency was almost worthless. But you don't want to hear that.
ANTONIO:	Why, why don't I want to hear that?
KAREENA:	Being from the west, you prefer ignorance.

Kareena resumes her walk, leaving Antonio behind.

SCENE FOUR

A tiny café, really just a cupboard with three tiny tables crushed into it. Costa, wearing a full length and soiled apron, sits on a tall stool and reads the paper. The English CBC radio morning show is playing in the background. When Jaroslaw enters Costa looks up and greets him.

COSTA:	Good morning my friend. The usual?

Jaroslaw nods, Costa pours coffee.

JAROSLAW:	Do you know any new jokes?
COSTA:	Sure! Absolutely! You come in here you should hear a new joke. That's the least you should get. Good coffee, a good laugh. But I have to ask you, this new joke, can it be one that you've heard before?

Jaroslaw smiles. François, a workmate, enters, and sits at the table with him.

FRANÇOIS: Hey, only one more day and then we're free.

JAROSLAW: Don't remind me.

FRANÇOIS: You'll find something. At least you have a degree.

JAROSLAW: It's worthless here. It's even more worthless there.

COSTA: What are you going to do, François?

FRANÇOIS: What about you, soon you'll have no customers left?

COSTA: Maybe if the government changes then the companies will stop moving out.

FRANÇOIS: It's got nothing to do with the government, not really. It's the condos. The building is worth more as a condo than as a warehouse. We're going to be unemployed because the times are good.

COSTA: Why is it that people who live in condos don't like my restaurant? They move in, they come once, but they don't come back.

FRANÇOIS: Costa, this isn't exactly upscale. They want to feel good about themselves, they come here, they wonder what they did wrong with their lives. You know what I mean?

COSTA: My sandwiches are good.

FRANÇOIS: Do you serve eggplant sandwiches?

COSTA: Who the hell wants to eat eggplant sandwiches?

FRANÇOIS: You eat an eggplant sandwich, you think, look, I've made a choice, I'm different. Does this restaurant do that to people? Does it make them feel different, in control?

JAROSLAW: I hate it when you feel something is inevitable, and
              then it happens. I hate that.

Costa and François look at him silently.

JAROSLAW: *(Quietly)* François, when are you going to tell
              your wife?

FRANÇOIS: I told her.

JAROSLAW: Really?

FRANÇOIS: *(Whispering)* I told her quietly, softly softly, like
              this, while she was fast asleep.

They all laugh.

FRANÇOIS: Have you told your sister?

JAROSLAW: No, not yet. Soon.

SCENE FIVE

*Kareena returns home. She places her grocery bags in the kitchen and
then enters her room. She takes off her shawl and, thinking better of
it, puts it over her head, as her mother wore it. She looks in the mirror,
then takes her chair, places it in the middle of the room, and sits.*

Petrov appears in the room.

PETROV: Were you followed?

MOTHER: No, of course not.

PETROV: How are your children?

MOTHER: I left them on the swings in front of the building.
              They are such wonderful children, and they play so
              beautifully together. I can't stay long, Petrov.

PETROV: They're well?

MOTHER: I think they are very well. They are perfect.

PETROV: The language they speak is threatened. The country
             of their birth is occupied. The memories of their
             ancestors are scorned. And yet, miraculously, these
             children are well, in fact, they are perfect.

MOTHER: What do you want from me, Petrov? Why did you
             ask me here?

PETROV: How old are they now? The children …

MOTHER: Kareena just turned six.

PETROV: And your boy?

MOTHER: Jaroslaw is four.

PETROV: I was thinking that you must miss your husband.
             You must wish he were here, to see them grow.

MOTHER: It was you who told me he was dead. You told me,
             in this office. I refused to believe you. I still refuse.

PETROV: Yes, I told you he had died. And that he had died
             for a good cause. I told you he was a hero.

MOTHER: If I remember correctly, you referred to his death
             as a necessary cost.

PETROV: Change never comes easily.

MOTHER: Is that your lesson for the day?

PETROV: But maybe I had to say what I did to help you.
             Maybe your ignorance and my deceit were necessary.

MOTHER: Say what you want to say, Petrov. Just say it!

PETROV: Victor is alive. He wants, very much, to see you again.

MOTHER: Do you mean what you are saying? Do you know
             what you are saying?

PETROV:	I told you he was dead because he asked me to.
MOTHER:	Alive. Petrov, is he alive? Is it possible to see him?
PETROV:	Not yet. There are things we must do.
MOTHER:	What do we have to do?
PETROV:	We know who betrayed Victor. He, too, is still alive.
MOTHER:	Who?
PETROV:	We must get him out of the way.
MOTHER:	Out of the way?
PETROV:	What do traitors deserve? Consider it carefully. Take your time. We will talk again.

The lighting changes, Kareena is clearly alone in her apartment, sitting on the chair, dressed in the shawl she associates with her mother, which she removes, folds, and puts away.

SCENE SIX

Kareena is using a knife to cut the fresh ingredients for a salad. Jaroslaw enters and looks at the mail on the table. He picks up an envelope.

JAROSLAW:	It's from Elections Quebec. They still haven't spelled my name right. Why didn't I just tell them my name was Jerry?
KAREENA:	Because it's not Jerry.

Jaroslaw picks a piece of tomato out of the salad and sits at the table.

JAROSLAW:	If I show up with my identification, but I'm on the list with the wrong spelling, can I still vote?

KAREENA: I don't know. The landlord called and said we were late with the rent. He said he'd come by tomorrow to pick up the cheque.

JAROSLAW: We have to give him something.

KAREENA: Can't we ask for a delay?

JAROSLAW: Maybe if we give him half.

KAREENA: Let's do that.

JAROSLAW: One more day and that's it, Kareena, the next cheque will be our last.

KAREENA: You'll find something.

JAROSLAW: Not soon enough.

KAREENA: Everything is going to be okay.

JAROSLAW: You promise?

KAREENA: Yes.

JAROSLAW: At least one of us knows the future. Too bad it's the crazy one.

Jaroslaw goes to the door.

KAREENA: Where are you going?

JAROSLAW: To Nicole's.

KAREENA: Why? You just got in, and I'm making a special supper.

JAROSLAW: I need to see her.

KAREENA: Are you coming home?

JAROSLAW: Not if I'm lucky.

SCENE SEVEN

Nicole answers opens her door to find Jaroslaw. She is pleasantly surprised to see him.

JAROSLAW: Sorry I didn't call first, Nicole, but I …

NICOLE: No, your timing is perfect. Olivier's gone with his father. He just left. He won't be back until Sunday.

He tentatively kisses her. She generously responds and he laughs with pleasure. Nicole smiles. Jaroslaw begins to undress her in a measured, somewhat teasing way, although soon they are both bursting with need and desire.

SCENE EIGHT

Kareena and Antonio stand at the edge of the river.

ANTONIO: I didn't expect to see you again.

KAREENA: What do you do?

ANTONIO: I'm a teacher, was a teacher. I took early retirement.

KAREENA: That's what you do?

ANTONIO: I go for walks, work in my garden. I bother no one and think the thoughts of an old socialist.

KAREENA: That's the only kind left.

ANTONIO: What?

KAREENA: Socialists, old. The only kind left.

ANTONIO: (Laughs) That's true. The young ones don't use that word any more. They found a new name for it. They call it green, now, don't they?

KAREENA: I don't know. Are you from Montreal?

ANTONIO: Not originally. Italy, southern Italy. My parents both died during the war and an uncle arranged for me to come here. I was seventeen. I worked as a gardener, studied, became a teacher.

KAREENA: What do you call it when someone says you share something, but they make all the decisions?

ANTONIO: I don't know, hypocrisy, a lie.

KAREENA: It was the socialists who imprisoned us, ruined the environment, made all the decisions, and called their system equality.

ANTONIO: That was totalitarianism. Not socialism. Big difference.

KAREENA: You think if we change the words then it didn't happen?

ANTONIO: I didn't mean that.

KAREENA: They called it socialism. That's the word they used.

ANTONIO: I'm aware of that. Do you think your country is better off now? I read that unemployment is back, child poverty is up, tuberculosis is spreading, pensions are worthless. I'm sorry, I shouldn't be so bleak, apparently organized crime is doing very well.

KAREENA: Very well. In fact, it is the government.

ANTONIO: You don't like the socialists, you don't like the capitalists. You're in a tough place, aren't you?

KAREENA:	Yes.
ANTONIO:	At least I have beliefs.
KAREENA:	That you believe in, or that you want to believe in?
ANTONIO:	I'm not saying I know the truth.
KAREENA:	Not beliefs then. Hopes.

SCENE NINE

Nicole and Jaroslaw are in a little but very busy restaurant on rue Duluth. We hear the sounds of a tacky Italian music track and the dishes and voices of neighbouring tables. Jaroslaw fills the glasses from a wine bottle he has brought with him. Nicole puts the glass to her lips and takes a sip.

NICOLE:	God! How can you drink this stuff?
JAROSLAW:	It gets easier the more you do it.
NICOLE:	You sure it's not paint remover?
JAROSLAW:	It's a lie remover. You drink it and layer by layer you discover the truth.
NICOLE:	I doubt that. But we can try.
JAROSLAW:	It loosens us up.
NICOLE:	You've never needed to loosen me up.
JAROSLAW:	Do you think you could get me a job with the government?
NICOLE:	No.
JAROSLAW:	Why not? Do I have bad breath or something?

NICOLE: You don't have the right skills.

JAROSLAW: What do you mean? I can waste time, pretend to
             work when I have to, tell people to call another
             number, what else do I need?

NICOLE: Great attitude.

JAROSLAW: Seriously.

NICOLE: You don't even speak the official language.

JAROSLAW: That's the point, why is there only one official
             language?

NICOLE: What, you want Ukrainian to be an official
             language of Quebec?

JAROSLAW: That's the problem, right there, you think of me
             as Ukrainian. You should just think of me as a
             western man.

NICOLE: How are you a western man?

JAROSLAW: When I first came to Canada—

NICOLE: Quebec.

JAROSLAW: I used to love watching people use credit cards. All
             they had to do was sign their names.

NICOLE: So?

JAROSLAW: Just sign their name. A small flick of the wrist.

NICOLE: And?

JAROSLAW: I owe the limit.

NICOLE: Is that how you define a western man? Someone
             who owes the limit. Congratulations! Now you pay
             interest on the interest.

JAROSLAW: What's wrong with that? How do you think people
               would buy without credit? And if they don't buy how
               is the economy going to grow, and if the economy
               isn't growing, then what will happen to our freedom?
               (Spontaneous yell) Credit makes us free!

*Nicole is embarrassed by just how much attention the outburst
receives, as other tables laugh and stare.*

NICOLE: Jerry!

SCENE TEN

Kareena is in her room. Petrov is with her.

PETROV: Victor is anxious to see you.

MOTHER: I haven't told the children anything. I wanted to tell
               them, but I haven't. It will be such a surprise.

PETROV: Everything we do is for their sake.

MOTHER: How is he?

PETROV: He has lost some teeth, some hair, but he is fine.

MOTHER: Where is he?

PETROV: Are you ready to help me?

MOTHER: Yes.

PETROV: Can you do what has to be done?

MOTHER: You asked me what a traitor deserved.

PETROV: And? Are you capable of it?

MOTHER: Yes.

Jaroslaw and Nicole are entering the apartment in a slightly drunken state. Jaroslaw still has the wine bottle in his hand.

JAROSLAW: Kareena! Kareena! Are you here?

KAREENA: Petrov, I need to know who. Who is it?

PETROV: I will tell you when it is time. It is a person you know well. I have to be careful, I have to take one small step at a time.

JAROSLAW: I'm sure she's here. She's always here.

Jaroslaw puts the bottle on the table. Nicole remains at the door, unsure whether to enter. Kareena enters from her room into the kitchen.

NICOLE: Hello.

JAROSLAW: Have you eaten? We went out for dinner. We went to one of those places where you can bring your own bottle. Do you want to smell it?

NICOLE: He filled an empty bottle with vodka and called it white wine.

JAROSLAW: A bit more kick for the money. Are you going to say something?

NICOLE: She doesn't have to say anything.

JAROSLAW: It's rude of her not to say anything. She does it to drive me crazy. Sometimes she goes whole weeks without talking. Other times she's angry because she says I won't talk to her.

NICOLE: Just because she doesn't talk doesn't mean she can't hear. How are you Kareena?

JAROSLAW: Are you going to answer?

NICOLE:	Leave her alone. It was your brother's last day of work today so we celebrated. It's no use everyone getting depressed.
JAROSLAW:	We're trying to stay positive.
KAREENA:	Our mother made a promise.
JAROSLAW:	She speaks!
NICOLE:	What do you mean, Kareena?
KAREENA:	I'd like some of your vodka.
NICOLE:	I thought your mother was dead.
JAROSLAW:	She is.
KAREENA:	She promised to kill someone. There is a traitor among them. Petrov will tell her who that is, and then … *(drinking)* Vodka should be cold.
NICOLE:	Who is Petrov?
JAROSLAW:	He was a friend of my father's. They all worked in the movement together. After independence he became a big man in the government. Now he owns several businesses that used to belong to the state. He helped us come to Canada. He gave us the tickets. He had the connections.
NICOLE:	You keep in contact with him?
JAROSLAW:	He wanted us far away.
KAREENA:	I want to dance.
JAROSLAW:	Why are you doing this Kareena? You are talking like a fool, acting like a fool.
KAREENA:	Find yourself a gypsy, Nicole, my brother may be foreign, but he's not a gypsy. He's a coward.

JAROSLAW:	Coward? Why?
KAREENA:	Because you know nothing and like it that way. Clap. Help me to dance. I know our mother danced. Why don't you clap for me? Do you want to dance with me, Nicole? Can't your legs support your body?
NICOLE:	I don't hear any music.
KAREENA:	That's why we clap, to help us hear the music.
JAROSLAW:	Jesus, Kareena!
NICOLE:	All right, let's dance. Your brother will clap.
KAREENA:	Will he?
JAROSLAW:	Kiss me first.
KAREENA:	That's what I want to see. Some passion. Come on, Nicole, let's see the muscles in your legs.
NICOLE:	Show me the steps, Kareena.

Jaroslaw claps and Kareena and Nicole begin to dance. Kareena moves with a challenging sexuality. Jaroslaw watches her intently, as does Nicole. Jaroslaw begins to sing out loud and Kareena, still dancing, joins in the singing.

Nicole approaches Jaroslaw. Half drunk, sweaty, they are committed to their desire within the moment and move into the next room, leaving a singing, equally sweaty Kareena to herself.

We can hear the back of Nicole rhythmically banging against the wall as she and Jaroslaw make love standing up in the next room.

Kareena rubs the sweat off her forehead with her forearm. Then she uses the front of her shirt. She goes to the sink and splashes water on her face. She takes off her shirt and splashes water over her entire torso.

SCENE ELEVEN

Morning. Light comes into the kitchen. Kareena is making coffee and slicing oranges. The juice runs on her hand and she licks it off. We see her pour the coffee and foaming milk into three cups.

Kareena brings two cups and the plate of oranges into her brother's room, where Nicole and Jaroslaw are both asleep. She wakes them and gives them coffee. Jaroslaw hardly responds, Nicole smiles at her. Kareena keeps her eyes lowered. As usual, she opens the blinds, and light floods into the room.

Kareena exits the apartment.

NICOLE: Looks like a beautiful day.

JAROSLAW: Let's go for a drive.

NICOLE: We need a car. We need a red convertible.
            The wind blowing through our hair …

JAROSLAW: Yeah.

NICOLE: Do you think we could rent a convertible?

JAROSLAW: Why don't we steal one?

NICOLE: Of course. What was I thinking? Steal one.

JAROSLAW: Nothing else to do today. Do you think we'll need
            a gun?

NICOLE: Can you get a gun?

JAROSLAW: I should steal the gun and then steal the car. I have
            the whole day.

NICOLE: That's logical.

JAROSLAW: The convertible, a gun on the dashboard, the radio
            blasting out gospel, the wind in our hair, Sweet
            Baby Jesus, now this is America.

NICOLE: Sweet Baby Jesus. Just you and I against … what are we against?

JAROSLAW: The world, baby, against the world! Straight through the bad towns and the bad lands leaving – what are we leaving? – exhaust, wherever we go. We should get married.

NICOLE: Get married?!

JAROSLAW: What's wrong with that?

NICOLE: I thought we were escaping.

JAROSLAW: We can get married in Texas.

NICOLE: You're not working. I have a decent job working for the government. Maybe all you want is security.

JAROSLAW: Jesus, that's a terrible thing to say. I'm not saying it's not true, I'm just saying that it's a terrible thing to say.

NICOLE: Let's take a trip. I have three weeks' holiday coming up. We can drive far in three weeks.

JAROSLAW: Kareena can sit in the back, she won't mind.

NICOLE: Are you serious? Our three weeks of freedom and we bring your crazy sister?

JAROSLAW: I was just joking.

NICOLE: I think you were being serious.

JAROSLAW: If you hadn't minded, maybe.

NICOLE: I say I want to travel with you and first you say you want to get married and then you say you want to bring your crazy sister in the back seat.

JAROSLAW: When we get married she can be the witness.

NICOLE: Very funny.

JAROSLAW:	She's family. She's my only family.
NICOLE:	I didn't think about bringing my family. I was going to leave Olivier with my parents.
JAROSLAW:	That's different. Kareena is vulnerable.
NICOLE:	She's as tough as they come. You're blind to who she really is. Did you see her last night?
JAROSLAW:	If we take off and she hurts herself then I will never forgive myself.
NICOLE:	Hurts herself?
JAROSLAW:	People do that. It happens. They can't stand being alive.
NICOLE:	You can't think like that. You can't. That's blackmail. You have to free yourself from her.
JAROSLAW:	Now that's a word. Free. My parents wanted a free Ukraine and they both disappeared, but I escape to the land of the free where I dream of a red car and a gun, but now you tell me that all I need, really, to be free, is to abandon my crazy sister.
NICOLE:	What do you want?
JAROSLAW:	Commitment. I want to build my life on a few commitments. Commitments to other people, not to ideas. That's all I want.
NICOLE:	Are you sure?
JAROSLAW:	Yes.
NICOLE:	I thought you wanted a red convertible.
JAROSLAW:	The colour isn't important.

SCENE TWELVE

Antonio sits on a bench by the water reading a newspaper. Kareena approaches, wearing her shawl.

ANTONIO: Kareena. I was hoping I'd see you.

KAREENA: I came by yesterday.

ANTONIO: Did you?

KAREENA: But you weren't here.

ANTONIO: I must have already left for my garden.

KAREENA: Where's your garden?

ANTONIO: It's just tiny, a small little plot, part of a community garden. We could walk there. Would you like to see? It's not far.

KAREENA: Yes.

They get up and start walking.

ANTONIO: It's just on the other side of that school. The city wanted to tear it up and build a condominium, but the community protested and we still have it, for the time being anyway.

KAREENA: Antonio …

ANTONIO: Yes?

KAREENA: I don't really want to see your garden.

ANTONIO: Oh … I …

She takes his arm and they stop walking.

KAREENA: Kiss me.

ANTONIO: What?

KAREENA: I want you to kiss me. Kiss me again. You are gentle.

ANTONIO: Kareena … Kareena …

KAREENA: I am not ashamed of this.

SCENE THIRTEEN

Jaroslaw is at the door talking to the landlord.

JAROSLAW: It's only half of it.

LANDLORD: I see that. I have eyes. So what am I supposed to
             do, rent it to someone else every second day? Or
             would you prefer if you live here in the mornings
             and I rent it to someone else for the afternoons?

JAROSLAW: I'm going to get you the money.

LANDLORD: You still have your job?

JAROSLAW: Yeah, of course.

LANDLORD: So why are you here during the day when you
             should be at work?

JAROSLAW: I'm on the night shift now. It pays better.

LANDLORD: Good. That's good. I expected to speak to your
             crazy sister. You know she's crazy?

JAROSLAW: Why do you say that?

LANDLORD: She talks to herself.

JAROSLAW: It's not a crime.

LANDLORD: Since you introduce the subject, not paying your
             rent is a crime.

JAROSLAW: You'll get the rest soon.

LANDLORD: When?

JAROSLAW: End of the coming week. For sure. You can trust me.

SCENE FOURTEEN

Kareena and Antonio are lying naked on a bed in a small motel room.

KAREENA: I should dress.

ANTONIO: No. Not yet.

KAREENA: I should.

ANTONIO: Why?

KAREENA: Because we are talking.

Kareena gets out of bed, collects her clothes together and begins dressing with her back to Antonio.

ANTONIO: You can only talk with your clothes on?

KAREENA: Don't make fun of me.

ANTONIO: I didn't mean to make fun of you.

KAREENA: I tried to bring my whole self to you.

ANTONIO: Your back is beautiful.

KAREENA: Will you tell your wife? *(silence)* Will you?

ANTONIO: I don't know. This has never happened before. Do you believe me, that it's never happened before?

KAREENA: She will know anyhow. You've betrayed her.

ANTONIO: I feel terrible. I feel wonderful. Strange, isn't it? What are you doing? You aren't going, are you?

KAREENA: You've fucked me, what more do you want?

ANTONIO: What?

KAREENA: Isn't it the truth?

ANTONIO: No.

KAREENA: There's nothing wrong with fucking somebody.

ANTONIO: Please don't talk like that. Please.

KAREENA: Don't be pathetic.

ANTONIO: Why are you angry at me?

KAREENA: I'm not.

ANTONIO: Kareena? A minute ago we were holding each other.

KAREENA: You are becoming more ridiculous.

ANTONIO: But I thought, I mean, it was ...

KAREENA: It wasn't me making love to you. I was my mother. I was making love to a dead husband who had returned.

ANTONIO: I don't understand what you're saying. I don't understand. Kareena, it was you and I ...

KAREENA: That's why I could bring my whole self to you. It wasn't me. I was my mother.

ANTONIO: I don't believe it.

KAREENA: Then you're a fool.

ANTONIO: Kareena, what's going on?

KAREENA: I have to go. I can't stay.

ANTONIO: Why?

KAREENA: I hate you. I hate your need.

A stunned Antonio watches as Kareena walks out and leaves him alone.

SCENE FIFTEEN

Kareena enters her apartment, trembling with emotion.

She goes into her room. She takes off her jacket and shawl and solemnly folds them and puts them away, as if putting away a part of herself she can no longer face.

She goes back into the kitchen and notices that the icon is missing from its usual place over the table. She is stunned. She sits at the table, resigning herself to the unknown.

Jaroslaw enters, carrying a bag under his arm. Kareena watches him intently.

KAREENA: What are you doing?

JAROSLAW: I walked along Notre Dame Street. I visited all the antique stores. Each one.

KAREENA: Why?

JAROSLAW: Why, what do you mean why? How much do you think it's worth? Do you think it's worth a month's rent?

KAREENA: How can you think like that?

JAROSLAW: Not even. Not even a month.

KAREENA: We can't sell it.

JAROSLAW: Yes we can.

KAREENA: Borrow the money from Nicole.

JAROSLAW: I'm not a beggar.

KAREENA: But if she knew that you were trying to sell the only valuable thing we have, don't you think she'd want to lend you the money?

JAROSLAW: If it's that valuable how come I can't sell it?

KAREENA: Ask her.

JAROSLAW: I can't.

KAREENA: Are you going to move in with her?

JAROSLAW: The artist who did this thought it was … I don't know, something for eternity, but it's worth almost nothing.

KAREENA: You think it will work, you and Nicole?

JAROSLAW: Yes. Absolutely. You should sell this.

KAREENA: I don't want to. I want to keep it.

JAROSLAW: That's the point. They knew I wanted to sell it. They could smell me coming. But with you they'd see how difficult it is. With me, they see the hunger, with you they'd see the tears. They'd offer you more.

KAREENA: I don't want to.

JAROSLAW: Try, Kareena. Can't you try? We need to buy some time.

KAREENA: Are you going to have children with Nicole?

JAROSLAW: Yes.

KAREENA: Has she said that?

JAROSLAW: No, but …

KAREENA: Ask if she wants a child with you, just ask.

JAROSLAW: What are you trying to say?

KAREENA: You can't talk about money. You can't talk about children.

JAROSLAW: So?

KAREENA: We don't belong here. Don't you see that? Let's find some other place. Let's go together.

JAROSLAW: I can't do that.

KAREENA: We can make it somewhere else. It will be easier somewhere else.

JAROSLAW: No.

KAREENA: Slavko, we only have each other. If we lose that then we lose everything.

JAROSLAW: I just want you to sell the icon. That's all I want.

KAREENA: I can't.

JAROSLAW: You have to.

KAREENA: Will we use the money to go away?

JAROSLAW: No. I am going to make it work here. I want it to work here. Please, Kareena, please, do what I ask.

He puts the icon back in the bag and places it in Kareena's lap.

SCENE SIXTEEN

Antonio is bent over in his garden. He looks up and is surprised to see Kareena walking towards him. He stands and watches as she gets closer. She is carrying the bag with the icon in it.

KAREENA: Are you happy to see me again?

ANTONIO: Yes.

KAREENA: Did I hurt your feelings yesterday?

ANTONIO: Yes.

KAREENA: I'm sorry.

ANTONIO: Did you come to explain?

KAREENA: No. I didn't. I need some money.

ANTONIO: We all need money.

KAREENA: I don't want you to give me money for nothing.
I want you to buy something.

Kareena takes the icon carefully out of the bag. Shows it to him.

KAREENA: It's an icon.

ANTONIO: It's very beautiful.

KAREENA: It was my grandmother's. It was given to her during
the Great Famine. Well, it wasn't given to her,
she traded her last bit of food for it. She thought
she was going to die anyway, so why not have
something pretty to look at while she suffered?

ANTONIO: I can't take this from you.

KAREENA: Do you know about the Great Famine?

ANTONIO: Not very much.

KAREENA: My grandmother said that when she looked at this
icon, when she was in pain, it helped her to think
that suffering was natural, and not to be frightened.

ANTONIO: She must have been a remarkable woman.

KAREENA: There was food, I mean, there could have been
food, but it was taken away.

ANTONIO: What do you mean, taken away?

KAREENA: The government said that everyone would own
all the land together, and they set quotas for the
harvest, but they were set too high. The peasants
couldn't deliver what was expected so the army was

sent in to gather the grain. But when they didn't
get enough they took the grain that was saved for
the cattle, and still they didn't have enough, so
they took the seed grain saved for the spring, and
still they didn't have enough, so they entered the
homes and stole the flour, because they said that
the harvests must have been hoarded and hidden,
and that the peasants were criminals. Now there
was no food, neither for us nor the animals. And
winter came. At first, as it hit, our family, like all
families, traded the most valuable things for a little
meat, a chicken or a cat, and then for vegetables,
and soon no one would give up food for anything.
They boiled the leather of their shoes and belts,
and ate bark from the trees and grass from under
the snow. My grandmother said that you could tell
when someone was about to die because the lice
would leave the hair and seek warmth at the corner
of the eye or at the nostrils. There were no guards,
no daily beatings, just slow starvation.

ANTONIO: There's nothing I can say.

KAREENA: At least four million of my people died. Some say
as many as ten. But the outside world paid no
attention at all. They didn't care. They still don't.
(pause) Will you give me a thousand dollars for it?

ANTONIO: I can't. I'm sorry.

KAREENA: Don't you have the money?

ANTONIO: It's not only my money. There are two of us.
My wife and I. It's what we live on.

KAREENA: A savings? Don't you have a savings?

ANTONIO: It's not just for me to decide.

KAREENA: Did you tell your wife about us?

ANTONIO:	No.
KAREENA:	Will you?
ANTONIO:	I don't know.
KAREENA:	Do you want to be with me again?
ANTONIO:	Not that way, no.
KAREENA:	You didn't like it?
ANTONIO:	I did. Very much. More than I want to admit. But I have to live with myself. I want to like who I am.
KAREENA:	Keep the icon. It belongs to you. I know that now. I'm not good enough for it. I'm not. You keep it. I'm giving it to you.
ANTONIO:	Do you want me to sell it for you?
KAREENA:	No. Just keep it. It belongs to you.

Kareena leaves abruptly. Antonio stares out in front of him. He looks beaten. He looks down at the icon and gently examines its surface.

SCENE SEVENTEEN

Kareena is in her room in her mother's persona. Petrov is with her.

PETROV:	Can you slip a blade into someone's heart while he sleeps?
MOTHER:	Petrov, who …
PETROV:	You are close to him.
MOTHER:	What do you mean?
PETROV:	Don't be ashamed. I won't tell Victor that you have a lover.

MOTHER:	How did you know?
PETROV:	I see everything.
MOTHER:	You think that man, the one I sometimes meet, in my loneliness, in my … need, do you think he is the traitor?
PETROV:	We know so.
MOTHER:	It's not possible.
PETROV:	Why not? He doesn't believe what you believe.
MOTHER:	That doesn't make him a traitor.
PETROV:	If you share our convictions then do what we ask.
MOTHER:	I have loved him.
PETROV:	Is that what you call it? Love? Licking the sweat off a stranger?
MOTHER:	I enjoy the sweat of strangers.
PETROV:	Don't you want to see your husband again?

Jaroslaw knocks on her door.

JAROSLAW:	Kareena? I need to talk to you. Let me in.
PETROV:	Can you do it?
JAROSLAW:	Kareena, let me in.
PETROV:	You can get close to him, you can lie beside him. When he is asleep, when he is vulnerable …
KAREENA:	What, Jaroslaw, what do you want?

Kareena lets her brother in. Petrov has disappeared.

JAROSLAW:	Who are you talking to?

KAREENA: I wasn't talking to anybody.

JAROSLAW: Have you sold the icon?

KAREENA: I took it to the man I told you about.

JAROSLAW: The old guy?

KAREENA: Yes.

JAROSLAW: And?

KAREENA: He has it.

JAROSLAW: Good. How much did he give you?

KAREENA: He said he couldn't afford it.

JAROSLAW: I'm confused. Did you sell it?

KAREENA: No.

JAROSLAW: But you're going to?

KAREENA: I don't have it anymore.

JAROSLAW: You just said you didn't sell it to him because he didn't have the money.

KAREENA: I said I gave it to him because he didn't have the money.

JAROSLAW: Jesus Christ! Kareena! What are we going to do for rent?

KAREENA: I'm glad I did it. We don't deserve the icon.

JAROSLAW: Give me his address and I'll go talk to him. I'll tell him about you, that you're crazy, he'll give it back.

KAREENA: Borrow some money from Nicole.

JAROSLAW: No.

KAREENA: Why are you betraying us?

JAROSLAW: Us? Who is us?

KAREENA:	Our people. You are betraying our people.
JAROSLAW:	Because I want to be happy with the woman I love? Then fine, you are right. I am betraying our people.
KAREENA:	Because you think you can deny who you are.
JAROSLAW:	I've never denied who I am! Never!
KAREENA:	You ignore our language, you ignore the sorrow of our parents, you don't care about our duties to them.
JAROSLAW:	Kareena, I'm talking rent!
KAREENA:	Because of rent we should betray their sorrows? Because of rent we should sell the icon to strangers? Because you can't talk to Nicole we have to sell it to just anybody?
JAROSLAW:	You always talk about our parents' sorrows, but you know nothing about them. You know nothing about their sorrows.
KAREENA:	At least I don't try to forget.
JAROSLAW:	You use their suffering to disguise your self disgust.
KAREENA:	What did you say?
JAROSLAW:	You heard me. They are just the excuse you use to reject your life and not to do something with it.
KAREENA:	Slavko, don't, that's cruel.
JAROSLAW:	When you met that old guy did you talk about our parents suffering, did you?
KAREENA:	Should I be ashamed of that?
JAROSLAW:	You should have told him you hate yourself, that you cling to the past because you hate.
KAREENA:	Don't be cruel.
JAROSLAW:	You think everyone but you is cruel, Kareena,

Kareena takes on the persona of her mother, to defend herself from Jaroslaw's accusations.

MOTHER: Why are you calling me Kareena?

JAROSLAW: Hide! That's it. Hide!

MOTHER: A son shouldn't talk like that to his mother.

JAROSLAW: Kareena.

MOTHER: I live only for my children.

JAROSLAW: You aren't her, admit that you aren't her!

MOTHER: Do you remember the songs I used to sing when you were little? I used to pour out my heart in lullabies. After Victor disappeared, I was so sad. It is almost comical how sad I was, how I gave myself to that feeling of loss. You don't remember your father, do you?

JAROSLAW: How could I remember him?

MOTHER: You were so little when he disappeared. You were just beginning to speak. You had learned the word papa, and after he left you used it for all sorts of things that made no sense: the chair was papa, shoes were papa, the door …

JAROSLAW: Yes, that's right, I called the door papa …

MOTHER: And then I met with Petrov.

JAROSLAW: What does he have to do with it?

MOTHER: He called me one day, told me that Victor was still alive. If I did what he asked, I would see my husband again.

JAROSLAW: Do you think that really happened?

MOTHER:	He asked if I was willing to kill the person who had betrayed my husband.
JAROSLAW:	Were you?
MOTHER:	Yes.
JAROSLAW:	Did you?
MOTHER:	I didn't know that the traitor had become my lover. How is that possible? How can such things happen?
JAROSLAW:	I don't know.
MOTHER:	And now I was to meet him, love him, and when he was asleep, to slip a knife into his heart. I went to the small hotel where we always met. I remember the moon as I walked there. It was rising in the sky, full of itself, so proud of its own beliefs. And I, too, was full, full of the tenderness I felt towards the husband I wanted to return. And then, holding on to that tenderness, I made love with the other.
JAROSLAW:	How could you do that?
MOTHER:	When he fell asleep, I was to kill him.
JAROSLAW:	Did you?
KAREENA:	Our mother is singing, do you hear her?
JAROSLAW:	Yes, I hear her.
KAREENA:	I hear her, too. I know it's only in my head, but it's so real, so sad. Our mother's voice is so sad.

ACT TWO

SCENE EIGHTEEN

Costa, in his apron, listens to the radio and reads the paper.
Jaroslaw sits at a table going through the Gazette. François enters,
looking uncomfortable in an ill fitting suit.

COSTA: Hey, hey, look who's here. I didn't recognize you.

FRANÇOIS: How could I stay away? I'm so used to your bad
food the good stuff gives me indigestion.

François joins Jaroslaw at his table.

FRANÇOIS: You're here, too.

JAROSLAW: It's not because of the food.

FRANÇOIS: Old habits die hard.

COSTA: What would you like, François?

FRANÇOIS: Coffee, sweet and black.

COSTA: Did you get a job with a computer company?

FRANÇOIS: What do you mean?

COSTA: The suit.

FRANÇOIS: They don't wear suits at a computer company.
They wear black T-shirts they have dry-cleaned. I
swear to God, they dry-clean their T-shirts. They
wouldn't be caught dead in a suit. It's only the
unemployed and politicians who wear suits. I told
my wife that.

COSTA: Politicians get good pensions. You won't see them
            working a grill when they get older.

JAROSLAW: They're advertising here for telemarketing jobs at
            the Gazette. Do you think I could do that?

COSTA: You know Alain? He used to do telephone sales.

FRANÇOIS: Who's he?

COSTA: You know the guy, he comes to visit now and then.
            Dips his cheeseburger into the soup.

FRANÇOIS: Oh him, yeah?

COSTA: He says he started out on the phones. They had
            a little office over there on St. Paul. Now he's an
            executive, office on René-Lévesque. He talks about
            his car. He talks about his secretary.

JAROSLAW: How hard can it be, make a few calls?

FRANÇOIS: We should try it, Jaroslaw. Sometimes it doesn't
            pay to think. We should just do it.

JAROSLAW: But I don't have the right clothes. Look at me.

FRANÇOIS: That's okay, it's telephone sales, nobody is going to
            care how you look. You could be naked for all they
            care, as long as you make the sales, as long as you
            fill your quota. Anyhow, I'm the one who looks like
            a retard. No-one trusts a guy in a suit.

COSTA: I think you look good, François. You remind me
            of my brother. He'd finish washing the dishes and
            then he'd put on his suit, a dark one in winter and
            a white one in the summer. Always. And he wore a
            hat, people wore hats then.

JAROSLAW: What happened to him?

COSTA: He stayed in Greece. I get a card from him
            at Christmas. I guess he's all right.

FRANÇOIS: You miss him?

COSTA: It's been years. How can you miss somebody
            after so many years?

SCENE NINETEEN

Jaroslaw enters his and Kareena's apartment.

JAROSLAW: Kareena? You here?

*Jaroslaw is aware of the emptiness of the apartment, its air of
loneliness. He moves softly and quietly. He sees where the icon used
to be and pauses. He sees a book on the table. At first he seems
disappointed, but when he sits and begins to read he obviously
enjoys himself. Kareena enters.*

KAREENA: Why are you here?

JAROSLAW: I live here.

KAREENA: You used to live here. Now you always stay with
            Nicole. Nice of you to visit.

JAROSLAW: Why'd you get him this? I told you to get him a toy
            or something. It's in Ukrainian, it's useless.

KAREENA: We used to own a book with that story when we
            were little. I remember reading it to you. I had to
            look all over to find it.

JAROSLAW: But it's supposed to be a gift for Olivier, not for you
            and me. It's his birthday.

KAREENA: You can read it to him. I thought you might like that.

JAROSLAW: Is there anything to eat?

KAREENA: Not much.

JAROSLAW: You don't keep food in the house?

KAREENA: You're never here.

JAROSLAW: So you don't eat?

KAREENA: We're going to a picnic, we don't need to eat now. Come on. You can read it on the bus. Nobody will know it's a kid's book.

SCENE TWENTY

Nicole and Jaroslaw are sitting at a picnic table. They are watching Kareena push Olivier on a new, brightly painted swing. He is calling out for her to push him higher. Kareena laughs with delight. We hear the ambient sounds of other children playing, and the occasional traffic.

NICOLE: Your sister is good with children. She really is.

JAROSLAW: Yeah, I suppose she is.

NICOLE: She should have a lover. Have children.
Why doesn't she have a lover?

JAROSLAW: I don't know.

NICOLE: Maybe she just doesn't tell you.

JAROSLAW: I applied for a job today.

NICOLE: That's great. Where?

JAROSLAW: At the Gazette.

NICOLE: You can't work for the Gazette! My friends are never going to understand if you work for the Gazette!

JAROSLAW:	It's just a job.
NICOLE:	It's an English rag. It's anti-Quebec. No, it's anti-intelligence, a conservative piece of propaganda shit!
JAROSLAW:	You're embarrassed. I embarrass you.
NICOLE:	That's not true. That's not what I meant. Anyhow, you can tell them that you quit.
JAROSLAW:	How can I quit if I don't even have the job? Besides, it's not like I'm editor-in-chief, it's just a telephone sales job.
NICOLE:	God! You can't go lower, convincing people to read the Gazette.
JAROSLAW:	They'd be paying me.
NICOLE:	I suppose someone has to do it.
JAROSLAW:	Do you think Olivier will like the book?
NICOLE:	I don't know.
JAROSLAW:	I used to love that story when I was little. It's very funny.
NICOLE:	But how's he supposed to know it's funny? The last time I talked to him he didn't read Ukrainian.
JAROSLAW:	The idea is that I read it to him, talk to him about it. Explain it, sort of. That's what I was thinking.
NICOLE:	The pictures are nice. And the thought is nice. He likes it when you spend time with him.
JAROSLAW:	I want us to have a child, Nicole. Wouldn't you like that, for us to have a child?
NICOLE:	Yes.
JAROSLAW:	Soon.

NICOLE:	Why soon?
JAROSLAW:	Because Olivier's still young and then they'll grow up together. They'll be close. Like a family.
NICOLE:	There's time Jaroslaw. I don't want to be pregnant right now. I'd have to go on maternity leave and …
JAROSLAW:	You mean I don't have a job.
NICOLE:	It's not the best time.
JAROSLAW:	I can't even pay my rent, let alone support you and a child.
NICOLE:	I didn't know you couldn't pay your rent. Why didn't you tell me?
JAROSLAW:	I didn't want to. I couldn't.

Nicole gets up to call Olivier.

NICOLE:	We should think about going. Olivier! Olivier!

Olivier slides off the swing and runs to his mother. Kareena comes up to Jaroslaw.

KAREENA:	Does this remind you of anything?
JAROSLAW:	No.
KAREENA:	When we were little. Our mother. You don't remember? Are you all right?
JAROSLAW:	I'm fine.
KAREENA:	I really enjoyed this.
JAROSLAW:	Nicole has to go out tonight. You can help me take care of Olivier. Why don't you come? What are you going to do at home alone?

KAREENA:	Some other time, Slavko, I promise.
JAROSLAW:	But now's a good time, a great time.
KAREENA:	I have to go home, I have things to do.

SCENE TWENTY-ONE

Kareena is taking tomatoes out of a brown bag while Antonio takes his jacket off and rests it over one of the chairs. He has also brought a bottle of wine.

ANTONIO:	They're from my garden.
KAREENA:	They smell so fresh.

Antonio looks around. He notices the nail on the wall.

ANTONIO:	I like your place.
KAREENA:	That's nice of you to say.
ANTONIO:	Is your brother here?
KAREENA:	He's never here.
ANTONIO:	Is that where the icon used to be?
KAREENA:	Yes. Where did you put it, in a closet?
ANTONIO:	No, I hung it on a wall.

Kareena washes a tomato and then puts it on a small cutting board on the table. She sits down and, with a sharp knife, slices it. Antonio sits down beside her.

ANTONIO:	I had a conversation with my wife. I told her how the picture got into your family.
KAREENA:	What did she say?

ANTONIO: She thinks I should have agreed to buy it.

KAREENA: But I gave it to you.

ANTONIO: Because you felt humiliated.

KAREENA: That wasn't it.

ANTONIO: We want to buy it. That's why I called.
That's why I'm here.

KAREENA: Are you serious?

ANTONIO: I have the money with me.

KAREENA: Should I take it?

ANTONIO: Of course.

KAREENA: I didn't expect this.

ANTONIO: I'm glad you're surprised.

KAREENA: I didn't force you to buy it, did I?

ANTONIO: No. I had refused, and have now reconsidered.
Please, take the money.

KAREENA: Thank you. Thank you. I can't believe it.

ANTONIO: It's good to see you smile.

KAREENA: I was thinking of my brother. For once he will
think that I've done something right. It's amazing
how this has worked out. It's perfect.

SCENE TWENTY-TWO

Nicole enters her apartment, where Jaroslaw has fallen asleep.

NICOLE: Jaroslaw. Wake up.

JAROSLAW: I fell asleep.

NICOLE: I see that.

JAROSLAW: I'm sorry.

NICOLE: There's no reason to be sorry.

JAROSLAW: I didn't mean to fall asleep.

NICOLE: Is Olivier all right? Did he go to bed on time?

JAROSLAW: Yes.

NICOLE: That's good. I was thinking about what you said, being short on rent.

JAROSLAW: I didn't mean to say anything.

NICOLE: Maybe you should move in here. Would you like that?

JAROSLAW: Why do you want to live with a man who is useless?

NICOLE: You're not useless.

JAROSLAW: I can't just move. I have a lease.

NICOLE: I realize that. Sublet it.

JAROSLAW: Kareena needs a place to live.

NICOLE: You have to let the inevitable happen.

JAROSLAW: What's the inevitable?

NICOLE: She has to find her own income, her own place. She shouldn't get the idea that life is a free ride. It isn't. She has to work to fit in. You try to fit in, god knows you try, so why can't she? She's healthy, you saw her this afternoon. She can work, even if its only taking care of children. You're not doing her any favours by letting her think she's above it all. Has she ever worked?

JAROSLAW: She used to work at a drycleaner's.

NICOLE: Maybe they'd hire her back. I'll pay the rent until the end of the lease but after that she's on her own. You should tell her that. *(Pause)* Do you want me to talk to her?

JAROSLAW: No. I'll talk to her.

Nicole reaches for her purse, takes out her chequebook and begins writing.

NICOLE: Just fill in the right amount, until the end of the lease. You can pay me back later.

JAROSLAW: It's not a lot. Three months.

He fills in an amount and returns it to Nicole.

NICOLE: You have to talk to her.

JAROSLAW: Nicole, you do want another child, don't you?

NICOLE: Don't rush me.

JAROSLAW: I just want to know.

NICOLE: I said not to rush me.

She tears the cheque from the book and gives it to Jaroslaw who takes it, gets up and begins to leave.

JAROSLAW: It's a good night's work for a baby-sitter.

NICOLE: What did you just say?

JAROSLAW: I said thank you.

NICOLE: That's not what you said.

JAROSLAW: It's better if I go now.

NICOLE: I don't want you to go.

JAROSLAW: I need to clear my head.

NICOLE: Why are you angry? I can see why I would be angry, but what right do you have to be angry?

JAROSLAW: I'm not. I'm sorry. Thank you for the money.

SCENE TWENTY-THREE

Jaroslaw is on his way home. As he gets closer he stops at the automatic banking machine to cash the cheque he received from Nicole. He enters the cubicle, puts in his card and completes the transaction. He pockets the cash.

Jaroslaw leaves the bank machine, hesitates, and then is attracted by the sounds of a bar. He enters it. We immediately hear the muted but chaotic sounds of a television, bar music, and the video lottery terminals.

An older woman with thin shoulders and thin dyed-blond hair is dancing slowly and alone on the dance floor.

Jaroslaw ignores her and goes to the bar and orders two vodka shooters, which he pays for with cash. He takes the drinks and sits at a small, somewhat garishly lit table. He downs one of the shooters as he watches the woman dance. Her movements are neither sophisticated nor difficult, but there is something alluring in her mix of concentration and freedom.

She notices him watching and smiles at him, and twirls for his behalf. Jaroslaw smiles innocently. She stops and speaks to him.

BAR WOMAN: You're not laughing at me, are you? (*Jaroslaw nods his head no*) I don't care if you laugh. You can laugh if you want. It's good to laugh. Do you like my dance? (*Jaroslaw nods his head yes*) You're a good boy. (*She points at the remaining shooter*) Are you saving that one for me?

JAROSLAW: Sure.

The woman sits down beside him and downs the shot.

BAR WOMAN: That's good. Cold and good.

Jaroslaw gets up and walks to the bar.

BARTENDER: Found yourself a girlfriend?

JAROSLAW: She's harmless.

BARTENDER: How many?

JAROSLAW: I guess four. They go down fast.

SCENE TWENTY-FOUR

Antonio and Kareena are finishing eating a salad and drinking the wine.

ANTONIO: I think you are a remarkable person.

KAREENA: Why do you say that?

ANTONIO: You make a great salad.

KAREENA: Did you tell your wife about us?

ANTONIO: No. What good would that do?

KAREENA: It would be honest.

ANTONIO: It would just hurt her.

KAREENA: Why don't you think she'd understand, like she did with the icon? *(pause)* Sometimes I want to stand on the street, hold out my arms and just let the wind take me somewhere.

ANTONIO: Why do you want to do that?

KAREENA: To lose all roots, all sense of the past.

ANTONIO: I would miss you.

KAREENA: You could talk to the icon.

ANTONIO: I don't think so.

KAREENA: Can you hear her singing?

ANTONIO: Who?

KAREENA: My mother.

ANTONIO: No.

KAREENA: Listen.

Kareena begins to accompany her mother. We only hear the one voice. Kareena stops singing. There is silence.

ANTONIO: I only heard you.

KAREENA: I can hardly remember her. Except her voice, I have so few memories of her, and I don't even know if those are true. Is that the right word, true? I remember she took my brother and I to swings in front of a big building. I remember that. It was strange, her taking us to that place and then leaving us alone. And I have this memory of her getting dressed in front of the mirror. She was putting on lipstick and she looked so pretty, and she smiled at me in the mirror. I remember that smile. Silly, isn't it, the things we remember are so small. So small. Soon after, she was found with a broken neck, lying at the bottom of steps. The funeral, I remember the funeral.

ANTONIO: Why did she die like that?

KAREENA: I don't know. I try to imagine.

ANTONIO: You can't imagine. You have to go back and ask the people who know.

KAREENA: Go into the village and gather my quota?

ANTONIO: I don't understand.

KAREENA: From each peasant gather a quota of memory, and when I have finished, when I have harvested all the memories, then I will have the truth.

ANTONIO: Yes, something like that. I think that's what I meant.

KAREENA: What if the memories are of betrayals that no-one wants to admit? How am I going to get my quota, Antonio? Do I insist that they know something different from what they tell me? Do I force it out of their closed mouths? And if the memories are in the minds of people who died, what then, do I dig up the bodies and see if they'll speak?

ANTONIO: That's not what I meant. You know that's not what I meant.

KAREENA: The truth belongs to everyone, oh yes, but someone else always decides how and when the quota is met. You'd have made a good Stalinist, Antonio.

ANTONIO: Don't insult me.

KAREENA: Maybe the past is an act of imagination. It's like forgiveness that way. Neither the past nor forgiveness can exist without someone imagining. Can you live with that, Antonio? Can you still breathe, knowing that's true?

ANTONIO: I don't understand what you said, what you are saying.

We hear Kareena's mother singing.

ANTONIO: Kareena?

KAREENA: You can't hear her?

ANTONIO: No.

KAREENA: It is so clear.

ANTONIO: I want to hold you. I shouldn't have said that.
I know you hate my needs.

KAREENA: I thought you wanted to like yourself.

ANTONIO: It must seem odd. I come, give you money and
ask to hold you, but it's not like that, you have
to believe me.

KAREENA: Will you leave right away after or will you stay?
Will you sleep with me?

ANTONIO: I could stay.

KAREENA: Would you like that, to sleep beside me?

ANTONIO: Yes, it would be beautiful.

SCENE TWENTY-FIVE

*Jaroslaw has returned to the table with the four shooters on a small
tray. He downs one of them.*

BAR WOMAN: Dancing keeps me young. That's what I think. It
doesn't keep me young in the face. I mean, look at
me. *(She laughs)* But it keeps the person inside of
me young. Do you want to dance with me, would
you like that?

Jaroslaw downs a second shooter. He stands.

BAR WOMAN: Where are you going?

JAROSLAW: Home. I should go home. But look, these two are for you.

BAR WOMAN: Don't you like the music?

JAROSLAW: It's okay.

BAR WOMAN: You're tense.

JAROSLAW: I can't relax.

BAR WOMAN: It's hard to let go sometimes.

JAROSLAW: That's right. That's fuckin' right.

BAR WOMAN: You have to relax.

JAROSLAW: I want to.

BAR WOMAN: Come here. Come over here.

The Bar Woman leads him into the darkened corridor behind the bar.

BAR WOMAN: Turn around, let me rub your back.

Jaroslaw lets her push him face up against the wall so that she can rub his back. She pushes hard and Jaroslaw starts to relax.

The Bar Woman pushes her body up against Jaroslaw. Her cheek is planted against his upper back, her hands continue a soothing motion along his sides.

She talks softly, as if to a nervous animal.

BAR WOMAN: Think of me the way I was. Can you do that? You can do that. I know you can. You have to imagine it, that's all. There is somebody you want, isn't there? When you turn around think of that person. That's who I am. Do you understand? All you have to do is to reach for her. Not yet, don't turn yet.

She continues to rub her hands on his back, down his thighs.

BAR WOMAN: Understand?

Jaroslaw, eyes still closed, nods agreement.

BAR WOMAN: All right. You can turn around now.

Jaroslaw turns and the old woman faces him. Jaroslaw opens his eyes and pushes himself away from her.

JAROSLAW: I have to go. My sister, my sister is waiting for me.

SCENE TWENTY-SIX

Kareena seems unsure of herself yet she stands and moves towards Antonio. She kisses him.

KAREENA: Do you think you could love me?

ANTONIO: I want to make you happy. That's what I want. Do you believe that?

KAREENA: Be gentle. Be tender.

She unbuttons her blouse. Antonio kisses her breasts.

ANTONIO: Your skin is so smooth.

KAREENA: What does it mean to betray someone?

ANTONIO: What did you say?

KAREENA: I asked what it means to love someone.

JAROSLAW ENTERS.

JAROSLAW: What the fuck is this?

KAREENA: Slavko!

Kareena starts to dress.

JAROSLAW: What the fuck are you doing?

KAREENA: It's Antonio. I told you about him.

JAROSLAW: The sick Socialist who stole the icon and wouldn't
              pay? Is this him?

ANTONIO: I didn't steal it! She gave it to me.

KAREENA: I gave it to him, you know that!

JAROSLAW: He's a thief, a pathetic thief.

KAREENA: No he's not. Besides, he decided to buy it.
              He's given me money. Look!

JAROSLAW: She's Ukrainian so she'll fuck anything for cash, is
              that what you think? He could be your father for
              Christ sake! Give him his filthy money back!

KAREENA: You don't understand, Slavko.

JAROSLAW: No, I never understand. I'm too stupid. Kareena,
              I have money. Nicole gave it to me. You don't have
              to do this.

KAREENA: That's not what happened.

JAROSLAW: Tell me he's not trying to fuck you! Go on! Tell me!

ANTONIO: The money is for the icon.

JAROSLAW: You shut up. You have nothing to do with it. You're
              a degenerate, that's all you are.

ANTONIO: You know nothing about me.

JAROSLAW: I know everything. Look around you. Look at the
              money. You think I don't know you?

ANTONIO: I don't have to put up with this.

JAROSLAW: You can't just walk away like that. You can't just
             fuck with us and walk out.

*Jaroslaw grabs Antonio and puts the knife that is on the table to his
neck. Kareena is both stunned and transfixed.*

KAREENA: What are you doing!

JAROSLAW: I just want to see some fear on his face.

ANTONIO: Please, don't. Please, you're hurting me.

JAROSLAW: Listen, he's begun to gurgle. What language is
             that? Italian? I can't understand you. Speak clearly.
             Speak good English!

*He pushes harder with the blade. A small amount of blood starts
to seep from beneath the blade.*

KAREENA: Don't!

JAROSLAW: Look at his eyes. He's frightened. Look at him.

*Kareena starts to hit Jaroslaw on the back. He grips Antonio
all the harder.*

KAREENA: Stop it!

JAROSLAW: Don't ever touch her again! Ever!

Jaroslaw pushes Antonio to the floor and steps away.

KAREENA: Why did you do that, Slavko, why?

JAROSLAW: He had it coming.

KAREENA: You should go! Just go!

JAROSLAW:	Come with me. I want us to go away.
KAREENA:	What?
JAROSLAW:	We need each other, you said that! If we lose each other we lose everything, you said that! Kareena!
KAREENA:	What about Nicole!
JAROSLAW:	She gave me money because she thought I'd leave you and move in with her.
KAREENA:	That's what you should do.
JAROSLAW:	Let's leave this city of lies. Let's both go! What's keeping you here? Nothing!
KAREENA:	I don't want to go, Slavko.
JAROSLAW:	You're the coward! You are!

Jaroslaw leaves. Kareena turns to Antonio.

KAREENA:	Are you okay?
ANTONIO:	He's a monster.
KAREENA:	He's not!
ANTONIO:	He wanted to kill me.
KAREENA:	He's not like that.
ANTONIO:	You don't know who he is.
KAREENA:	You should go.
ANTONIO:	You wanted me to stay.
KAREENA:	I was wrong.
ANTONIO:	I want to stay.
KAREENA:	Please go.

ANTONIO: We were close.

KAREENA: I didn't feel it.

ANTONIO: Don't do that. Don't deny what's between us.

KAREENA: You have no idea what's between us.

ANTONIO: You're wrong.

KAREENA: Go!

Antonio leaves. Petrov appears.

PETROV: You met with him again?

MOTHER: Yes.

PETROV: You slept with him?

MOTHER: No.

PETROV: Did you do what had to be done?

MOTHER: Yes.

PETROV: Good. I'm a bit surprised, but good.

MOTHER: Petrov, why does no one touch you? Many have
            had their lives ruined, jobs taken away, forced to
            move, or disappeared. But you, nothing.

PETROV: I am careful.

MOTHER: You are the best known, the most active, and yet
            no one touches you. Why is that?

PETROV: What are you trying to say?

MOTHER: How can we know who is betraying us?

PETROV: Did you kill him?

MOTHER: I told him to leave.

PETROV: You let him walk out? Do you think there won't be consequences? Do you?

MOTHER: I couldn't do it.

PETROV: I promised you the return of your husband, the return to your children of their father.

MOTHER: You promised me what I wanted to hear—kill the enemy and our dead will awaken. It's not true, is it Petrov? It's never been true. But if we believe then we are tools in your hand.

PETROV: You don't know what you're talking about.

MOTHER: Victor is gone, and I will never know how or why.

PETROV: You couldn't do what had to be done. Fine. You are a coward. I am sorry for your children. I am sure they will miss you. It's odd, isn't it, in life, how some can just walk away and others fall.

MOTHER: I am going back to my children.

PETROV: I trust my footing, my sense of balance, the friends I make and the arrangements I keep, but you, you might slip, stumble. God knows what might happen.

MOTHER: They need me. No matter what you do, you will never separate us. You can't separate us.

The Mother begins to descend the stairs. Petrov nods to several men who emerge from the shadows. Just before they grab her she stumbles and falls, ending sprawled and unmoving at the bottom of the steps, her head resting at an unusual angle to her body.

There is a slight sound of breathing. The last image in the scene is of Kareena alone, sitting in her chair in her room, staring straight in front of her.

SCENE TWENTY-SEVEN

Antonio sees Jaroslaw on the street and, after an initial hesitation, gathers his courage to talk to him. Jaroslaw looks at him as if he has more important thoughts on his mind.

ANTONIO: You frightened me.

JAROSLAW: So?

ANTONIO: You frightened me with a knife, but I am not afraid of you.

JAROSLAW: You see up there, in the sky?

ANTONIO: What?

JAROSLAW: The moon. We call it the moon, but maybe it's not. Maybe we're standing at the bottom of the Black Sea, the water is above us for miles and miles, and way up there, floating on the surface, is a boat with a huge searchlight. And the stars, the thousands of stars, they are other boats with searchlights, even further away, and all these people with searchlights on the boats are trying to see to the very bottom of the Black Sea. They want to see everything, know everything. They even want to see you and me. That's amazing, isn't it? And do you know why? Because they think that if they can see it all, they will know what is inevitable. That's funny.

ANTONIO: What's funny about it?

JAROSLAW: Why would anybody want to know what's inevitable?

Jaroslaw laughs.

ANTONIO: I'm not laughing.

JAROSLAW: You don't see the humour?

Antonio walks away.

JAROSLAW: Antonio!

Antonio turns. Jaroslaw pulls the knife that he had used to threaten him from out of his pocket. He holds it up to reflect the light.

JAROSLAW: I know who betrayed Kareena. And I will kill him.

SCENE TWENTY-EIGHT

Kareena comes out to meet Jaroslaw.

JAROSLAW: I don't feel so good. I feel like I have a big stone in my stomach, and I feel like my heart is burning, and everywhere in my whole body I feel this wrongness that just goes around and around, around and around, around and around. I keep waiting for it to go away, but it only gets worse. I want to let it out, let all the wrongness pour out.

KAREENA: Sssh! Don't talk like that.

JAROSLAW: How do I let it out? How do I let it go?

KAREENA: I love you, Slavko. I'll always love you.

JAROSLAW: You're so beautiful. It bothers me how beautiful you are.

KAREENA: Go and give Nicole back the money. You'll feel better. Tell her you don't need it. Tell her we sold the icon. Let her know you are strong, that you can make sacrifices.

JAROSLAW: Is that what you want me to do?

KAREENA: Yes. Think of our parents. The kind of choices they
             faced. How tough they were.

JAROSLAW: We know nothing about them.

KAREENA: Yes, we do ... I do.

JAROSLAW: No, you don't. You don't. You live in a world of
             made up possibilities and call them memories.

KAREENA: Don't say that, Slavko. Don't.

JAROSLAW: And you talk as if these possibilities will give
             you some important insight that will change
             everything. What message is the past going to give
             you, Kareena? What can the past possibly tell you
             that means something?

KAREENA: Go back to Nicole.

JAROSLAW: Answer me, Kareena, what does the past say?

KAREENA: You'll feel better after you give the money back.

JAROSLAW: I want to travel. I want to go far.

KAREENA: Promise me you'll go back to her.

JAROSLAW: Go home, Kareena. You go home. I'll do what has
             to be done.

KAREENA: You'll go?

JAROSLAW: Yes, I'll go.

*Kareena leaves Jaroslaw. Jaroslaw plunges the knife into his own
neck and crumples on the sidewalk. During the following the sound
of breathing ebbs and stops.*

*The bartender comes outside. He comes upon Jaroslaw lying on
the sidewalk. A pool of blood has formed around his head and
shoulders. The knife is beside him. The bartender enters the bar
and, in no great rush, walks to the phone behind the bar. He dials*

three digits, waits briefly, then can be seen talking. The old woman, as before, is slowly dancing by herself.

We hear sirens as the ambulance approaches.

SCENE TWENTY-NINE

It is day. François and a very subdued Costa sit at a tiny table.

FRANÇOIS: They brought him to the hospital, but he didn't make it. He died that night.

COSTA: Why? Why?

FRANÇOIS: I don't know. I went to his house the next day, thinking we'd go together for the job. I saw his sister. Tears kept streaming down her face. She could barely talk. The funeral is tomorrow.

Costa stands up, gets a menu and returns to the table.

COSTA: Have you seen the new menu?

FRANÇOIS: No.

COSTA: I don't call the omelette an omelette any more. I call it a fritatta. It's the same thing with hot sauce.

FRANÇOIS: Serious?

COSTA: And I offer eggplant sandwiches. See? I think it was you who suggested that.

FRANÇOIS: Jesus, Costa, who eats those? I was only joking.

COSTA: No, you were right. The people from the condos will like it. I even bought three different kinds of olive oil, so they feel they have a choice. They'll really love that. *(Pause)* I'd like to go with you, to the funeral. I want to say good-bye.

255   *Kareena*

SCENE THIRTY

A modest, small room, with a vase of flowers. In the middle of the room stands a silently weeping Nicole. Costa and François stand together, awkward in their suits, at a slight distance. Neither Olivier nor Antonio are there.

There is a small choir of mostly older Ukrainian woman who are gathered in front of the closed coffin which can barely be seen through their bodies.

Kareena is near the front. She is still, seemingly unmoved.

The lead singer begins the line, and the rest of the women join in. There is a surprising resilience and beauty in their voices.

François and Nicole share a brief and murmured exchange.

NICOLE: I thought maybe you could tell me something that would help me to understand.

FRANÇOIS: No. I'm sorry.

As Kareena watches, the lighting shifts and her younger self with her younger brother enter the room. They stand quietly as at their mother's funeral. Petrov, too, enters. He approaches the children.

PETROV: You must be her children. She often talked of you. I want to tell you how sorry I am. I'm so very sorry. I knew your mother well. I thought very highly of her. Everything we did together, everything, was to improve the world for you, the children. If I can ever be of help, just ask.

Petrov disappears, leaving the young brother and sister holding each other's hands. The young Kareena and Kareena stare at each other. Then the children also disappear. Kareena is again present at

*the small funeral for her brother. She finds her voice and begins to
sing, joining with the voices of the other women.*

SCENE THIRTY-ONE

*Nicole is sitting alone at a picnic table by swings. She sees Kareena
coming to meet her and gets up to greet her.*

NICOLE: Thank you for meeting me. I wanted to see you. I
would have gone to your apartment but I thought
it might be nicer if we met here. I haven't seen you
for a while. I think about you. I have conversations
with you in my head.

*Kareena opens a thermos that she has brought with her and pours
coffee for the two of them.*

NICOLE: I hurt very much and I think the only person who
might understand is you. You must hurt very much.
Aren't you going to speak to me? Can't we talk?

KAREENA: Tell me that the coffee is good.

NICOLE: The coffee is good.

KAREENA: Thank you.

NICOLE: I opened my heart to him. Was that wrong? I
offered to share my life with him. Was that wrong?

KAREENA: It's not your fault.

NICOLE: No. Will you go back to Ukraine?

KAREENA: No.

NICOLE: You'll stay?

KAREENA: Yes. Why didn't Olivier come to the funeral?

NICOLE: I haven't told him what happened. I told him that Jaroslaw went home.

KAREENA: Went home?

NICOLE: To Ukraine.

KAREENA: Montreal was his home.

NICOLE: You know what I mean.

KAREENA: No, I don't know what you mean.

NICOLE: I lied to him, okay? I lied to him. I just want him to forget.

KAREENA: To forget?

NICOLE: Do you want to stay with me for a while?

KAREENA: I wouldn't lie to Olivier. You have to know that.

NICOLE: What would you tell him?

KAREENA: My mother and father were never real to us. Never. They have always been hidden, and its not the six feet of dirt that hides them, but lies. Each of them lies buried beneath six feet of lies.

NICOLE: I can tell Olivier. I'll find a way to tell him.

KAREENA: Nicole, I know that Jaroslaw loved you. I know he loved you very much.

NICOLE: Are you just saying that?

KAREENA: No. He wanted to start again, with you. It's what he really wanted. I know that.

Nicole and Kareena remain seated, side by side, sipping coffee.

KÜT: SHOCK AND AWE

────────

The influence is P'ansori. One performer speaks for all the characters and shares the stage with a single musician. There are no objects on stage other than the musical instruments to be used.

There is, however, no musical accompaniment during the American friend's first monologue, delivered directly to the audience.

First Movement: Sonata Allegro

The American Friend

I am glad to be here, in Korea, visiting you. Thank you for letting me stay with you. It is a privilege.

Your husband, my friend, has been dead almost a year, and I very much wanted to be here during this time of remembrance. I have often thought of him.

As you know we first met in Vietnam. A long time ago. Few Americans realize that the South Koreans fought beside us in that war but I, of course, I never forget. We were both young soldiers then. It's amazing how easily those words slide together: young, soldier. Neither of us was conscripted: we both volunteered, he for his country and I for mine, and we fought together, side by side.

I believed in it then. The cause. At the beginning, I believed in all the arguments for why we were there, that somehow I was doing what was necessary for freedom and independence, maybe not of my own people, but for a weaker people who had asked us to come. I thought we were doing the noble thing, the generous thing.

I remember we were sitting in a field beside a small village whose name ... I can't remember, and we were both covered in sweat, and the sky above us was grey and laden, and it looked as if it was about to open and wash us with rain, which would have been welcomed, it had been a long day. We were waiting for the chopper to take us back to the base and your husband was looking around, or maybe looking inside, I don't know which, and he said, simple like this, he said, 'the real is good'. Just like that, 'the real is good.'

I remember leaning forward and saying to him: 'That's a question, not a statement. It's a question.'

After the war I wanted to know what had happened to him, what he was thinking, how he was. I didn't have his address so I sent a letter to him just 'Care of the Korean Army'. He got the letter. He was surprised to get it, but that's how our correspondence began. His broken English got better and better and my lack of Korean never changed. Eventually he came to visit me in Arizona, not that long ago. Of course, you know that. I don't really know how he felt about my country, but we, we were relaxed together.

While I am here, I want to visit some of the famous Buddhist monasteries I have read so much about. I look forward to that. Soon, I will be out among your beautiful mountains trying to keep my back straight and my mind empty.

My understanding of Buddhism actually goes back to that time in Vietnam.

Your husband and I were involved in the Phoenix Project. I am not sure how much he ever told you about that. People don't want to talk about that kind of thing very much and frankly, I don't blame them. Our job was to pacify the countryside. Pacify. Bring peace to.

We were sent into certain places, towns, villages, hamlets, with instructions to 'remove obstacles'. That's how we put it. Makes it sound like we were some kind of engineers, doesn't it, or drove bulldozers, or were even heart surgeons … removing obstacles. In fact, we were members of an elite team whose express and only purpose was to kill collaborators, or people we thought were collaborators: those who pretended to be our friends during the day and proved to be our enemies at night.

We were good at it, your husband and I. We knew how to do what was asked, and to get out quickly and safely.

We would get a list of names, and our job was to make sure they didn't ever see the dawn again. I will be honest with you, it was kinder to kill the person quickly than to bring them back for interrogation. Almost no-one survived interrogation, and those who did would rather have died. No-one now seems to remember the tiger cages we kept. They have been erased from the history we tell. It's more than a failure of memory, it's part of an on-going design of ignorance.

The names on these lists of collaborators came from the interrogations. Can you imagine? When in extreme pain you give names. You give anyone's name, everyone's name. They tortured people to get a list of names of people who were tortured in turn only to get more lists. It's silly, really. It's happening now in Guantanamo, Baghram and countless other unnamed places … but I don't want to talk about that now … the point is, it's barbaric, doesn't work … still continues.

It used to bother me that I had killed the innocent as well as the guilty. It doesn't bother me anymore. Not that. I've thought more deeply about it. It's only conceit to pretend that there's a real distinction between the two. I mean, the guys in the airplanes dropping bombs don't try to hold on to that kind of distinction. How could they? And if the war was never justified in the first place, what can it possibly mean, the guilty? Seriously?

So let us say the obvious, we were not there to kill the guilty, we were there to kill all those who, for strategic reasons, were in the wrong place at the wrong time. We once supported Afghani fundamentalists and Osama against the Russians. We armed the Iraqi nationalists and Saddam against the Iranian fundamentalists. And now we swear that both are our mortal enemies. It's our strategic goals which determine their guilt or innocence.

It took me a while to understand that.

If one has killed a person, or many people, as I have, there is a certain questioning that gathers momentum in one's life. At first one wants to think of it in big sounding words: sin, redemption, justice. But really, it isn't like that at all. It's simpler, more about the nature of change. You come face to face with this great … discontinuity. Lives do not continue. People, things, places, even thoughts, really do disappear. We think we know that, but we don't. It's hard to know that.

And it's not only the world of the dead person which has changed, but the world of the person who killed as well. Before the action you have not committed it, and after you have and there's no going back. You can no more reach back to what was before than can the dead.

I think, too, that a country that organizes to kill or torture, afterwards it's no longer the same country. Oh, they would like us to believe it is, they desperately want to convince us that the change has only happened to the dead or the wounded, but they are wrong.

After our missions, we were injected with sodium pentothal. Some people call it the truth serum. We would get an injection. We were injected to make it impossible to shut up. That's what the drug would do. Not being drunk, worse, it was like not being in control of your own mind, even though your mind was still clear. Or seemed clear.

There would be three intelligence guys sitting in front of me asking questions. They called it a debriefing. Not that it was ever brief. I mean the whole purpose of the drug was to make sure I'd talk and talk. Chatter away. They'd ask what the weather was like and I'd go on about a particular shade of blue in the sky, if I had ever seen it before, and the clouds, the shapes of them, whether they reminded me of a duck, or a horse, or a Chinese dragon or an American eagle, and how high I thought they were, and they'd say enough about the weather … so I'd talk about the vegetation, strange plants I had never seen back home, myriads of greens, and the fuzzy underside of a leaf and how it felt when moist, and they, the intelligence guys, they would try to get me back on track, and I would nod, try to concentrate, and answer the next question.

But I'd feel kind of ill, too, because the drug, it wasn't natural, and my mouth would be dry and kind of woolly and they'd notice and would ask do you want a glass of water, and I'd say, yes, I would really like that. Thank you.

And then they'd get to the point and ask what all the guys each did and if the mission was a success. And I'd tell them about the jokes we told, and who laughed, and why I thought they thought it was funny and then I'd go on about the heaviness of the rifle, lugging it around, and the soreness of my shoulder, from the kickback, and then I'd tell them about the faces of the people that disappeared, so to speak.

Faces that exploded, more accurately … sometimes exploded in recognition that this was, in fact, their last moment, and sometimes … much more literally, just … exploded.

And the weird thing is, I wanted them, my interrogators, to like me. Can you imagine? I talked and talked about what I had done hoping they would like me, and they did like me, they would say, good, good, yes, you are a wonderful soldier, so daring, so aware.

I was the guy they would send out to the places they were too frightened to go, and do the work they were too high and mighty to do, and when I got back I would tell them everything. I was this incredibly sensitive recording device and when they injected, I spoke.

And it astonishes me to this day, it humiliates me, to this day, the incredible lack of dignity in being drugged to answer questions like that. I remember feeling a rage, like I never felt before, rage at being injected with something to give the details about actions which I never should have done, to say it and be recorded for all time front of three people who would never take responsibility for the blood I have on my hands at their request, and they were questioning me, asking me if I forgot something. Forgot something.

At my last debriefing I remember I leaned forward real fast and got one of them by the throat, my thumb in exactly in the right place, exactly the right place, and all I had to do, all I had to do, was just … twist it in the right way, and I swear to God …

That was the only time I ever fought for freedom and independence in Vietnam, and the only time I didn't kill when I should have.

I was kicked out of the military after that. I was forced to leave. Trauma, they said, stress, psychological problems. They were frightened of me. One of them called me a killer gone mad.

It's odd isn't it, it was exactly at that moment when I learned not to kill that they decided I was a killer gone mad. You see, its not what you actually do that makes you guilty, it's only where you fit within their strategy. They see nothing else. They are permanently, perfectly blind to everything other than their desire.

In any case I had learned something, I had learned that even with the thumb in the right place and the right motivation you don't have to do it. I had learned that there's an independence which comes from the act of not doing, and a freedom, a blessed freedom, which comes with silence.

What is particular to Korean Buddhism, at least as I know it, Seon Buddhism, is that revelation is not a series of words being strung together for us to repeat, it's not like the Christian creed that way. In fact, it's only when words stop that there's even the possibility of enlightenment. Only when we go beyond the spoken …

I believe, now, that it is the radical discontinuity of self which is the reality we ignore. We change. I am no longer that particular person, my younger self. That person is an illusion held together by chains of silly words spoken by people who refuse to live in the present. It is not who I am now.

So those words your husband spoke to me, the real is good,
I have interpreted them in my own way, to mean that, in the
present, there is a place of silence, of non-action, and within it
change, real change, is always taking place.

So it is with a tremendous amount of respect that I talk to you
tonight. I want to honour that man, your husband, who had such
an effect upon me, and I look forward to meeting his children to
tell them, too, how much I honour him.

Opening verse from hymn "Onward Christian Soldiers"
played pizzicato on the cello.

The Daughter

My mother has told me about your conversation with her. She is happy
you are here, and is very surprised how openly you spoke to her.

My mother has told me about your conversation with her. She
is sorry that her English isn't better, as she is afraid she didn't
understand all you wanted to say. She says that you carry a great
hurt inside you and that she hopes you will find some peace
while you are here. She welcomes you as a friend of my father.
She wishes that … she wishes that …

기닥

My mother has told me about your conversation with her and
how happy she is that you are here. She was surprised to learn
that you are not a Christian as we are a Christian family and
my father, as you must know, was devoted to the church. My
mother was Christian as a girl but my father only chose to
become so after he finished military service. We, my brother and
I, were both baptized. We were both born in a hospital founded
by missionaries, and both studied at universities founded by
missionaries. He at Yonsei, I at Ewha. It was an honour for us to go.

기닥닥

My mother has told me of your conversation. She wishes she had a better grasp of English but she is happy that you will have other conversations with her. She has been lonely over the past year, not because she doesn't have friends but rather, well … perhaps she has withdrawn a bit into herself since the death of my father. She should travel, I think, but she says it is too late, although surely it is never too late. I would like to travel … I have been to Japan, to China, briefly, but have never left Asia, but will, I think, perhaps to further my studies, I would like to do that but I have to work now and I keep my mother company. My brother is married and has children but rarely visits. I am not married. I don't expect to get married, although sometimes I wish I could have had … Perhaps, one day, my mother and I will travel together, that would be good, she and I on an airplane, or staying in a small hotel in …

닥, 기닥닥

Moses not only led his people out of slavery but gave them a set of laws to be applied equally to all. Freedom from foreign oppression and equality under the law – how could that not be attractive to us? We, so weakened by the fixed hierarchies of Confucian society and the passivity of Buddhism, had let ourselves become the slaves of another people. We were brutally occupied for 35 years, from 1910 until 1945, until the Japanese, our occupiers, were defeated by your country, a Christian nation, with Christian soldiers.

It is a bit odd, for us, my mother and I, to think that you, from America, see the same religion so differently. That is if my mother is right in what she says. I am not sure that she truly understood.

Of course, there is always a conflict between true Christians with their commitment to social justice and the centralizing might of Empires which claim Christ as their leader, but to whom faith is nothing but an organizing principle for propaganda. The Constantines of every age depend on lies and confusion. But as Christians we have the courage to turn our backs on the hypocrites; point out Bush, Blair, Rumsfeld, Cheney, Rice, witness the true intentions behind their pretend religion, the diseased flesh behind the masks of innocence. Do you think all Christians wrong because war criminals hide among us?

기닥

My mother has told me about your conversation with her. She is sorry that her English isn't better, as she is afraid she didn't understand all you wanted to say. She says that she hopes you will find some peace while you are here. She welcomes you as a friend of my father. She wants to say ... I want to say, that the enduring gift of Christianity is that it opens our eyes to the grace of a loving god who embraces all with a compassion that shines in all corners of the world and is available to each and every one of us. Let that light shine in your heart, to soothe and comfort you.

You need not pretend that you are another person from one moment to the next, or that the world only changes in silence, beyond our reach and understanding. Forgiveness will not be found through evasion, but in truth.

The American Friend

Forgiveness, did I hear the word forgiveness?

How often have I seen young soldiers bow their heads in fervent prayer in the vain hope that the consequences of the deed will not cling to them. They will be forgiven.

I have done it myself.

All that *divine* forgiveness really means, or has ever meant, is that the guilty, if they are of the right group, go free. That's all it is. A touch convenient, isn't it?

You think Christianity is a radical search for social justice, rooted in a profound understanding of the will of the divine. Is that right? We are loved by a loving God and if only we could recognize that and acknowledge it and live according to it ... is that right?

At the end of both bibles, the Hebrew and the Christian, there is an apocalypse, a moment where all the enemies writhe in eternal pain, or have been turned into ash or dust, and the faithful, they rejoice. The whole world is on fire and the faithful sing praises. Hallelujah. That is the ultimate vision of your religion, what used to be my religion: victors dancing on the many corpses of their slain enemies. Is that too strong for you?

Do you have any sense of the true worth of the spiritual traditions which it has taken thousands of years for your people to achieve? Why are you abandoning those roots now? How can you be happy to do so? It pains me to see it.

Every time a religion declares that there is one and only one true god, that is a declaration of war against all those who believe in another. Does Confucianism do that? Buddhism? Taoism? It is the tradition of the militant west that claims one and only one true god, so that we can insist that *we* are the beloved of this benevolent god who will forgive, no, who will *bless* our crimes.

Let me ask you this, are you happy to see your people erase their own culture for the self-serving indoctrination of a movement whose ultimate vision is the total defeat and eradication of all its enemies?

따 구궁궁, 구궁궁, 구궁궁 따, 구궁궁, 구궁궁 따,
구궁궁, 구궁궁 따, 구궁궁, 구궁 궁

SECOND MOVEMENT: ANIRI P'ANSORI

The son has invited the American friend to a restaurant.

The Son

구궁 딱딱 궁, 구궁 딱딱 궁
구궁따따궁

We should eat. It is time to eat. Do you like Soju? [궁] It tastes
like a gentle vodka. We could try it. Are you comfortable?
[궁따] Ah, from meditation. Well, an unexpected benefit from
meditation, you can sit at a low table while drinking Soju. [따]

Did you know that Koreans use the spoon and the chopsticks
simultaneously? [궁따] And we use scissors, too, that surprises
westerners, but really, why not bring scissors to the table if they
are the right tool at the right time. We also drink from the bowl.
Sometimes the bowl itself is the right tool. Shall I order? [구궁따]

Down in Cholla, in the south, [중모리 *rhythmic cycle*] they have
incredible food. Everyone thinks so. Every side dish is a delicacy
and every delicacy is tastier than the last. I have had meals with
thirty side dishes. And when you're full, they come with the main
plates. But this will be good. May I? *[stop cycle]*

We never pour our own drink. We keep an eagle eye on the
other's glass and then refill it as soon as it is empty. [궁] And
when we pour we hold the other arm like this, as if to hold back a
large sleeve. [구궁] In our imagination we are all still aristocrats
and wear large, drooping sleeves. [구궁따] Thank you. To what
should we drink? To the spirit of my father? May he find peace.

It is usually quite hard to upset my sister but you went straight
for the jugular. [궁따] You told my sister that she was giving up
her Koreanness by being a Christian. That is what you meant,
isn't it? You are not the first to suggest it. The issue isn't whether
you were impolite. It's a fact you were impolite. The issue is that
you are ignorant as well as impolite.

Christianity first came to Korea through China. Three hundred
years ago. The Jesuit Mateo Ricci settled in Beijing from where
his influence spread. His beliefs were received as a particular
form of Confucianism. The son of heaven is a common term
for a Confucian sage, and has been for a very long time. What
sage worth his salt would not call himself a son of heaven? And
40 days alone in the wilderness is hardly long for a wandering

Buddhist monk. Jesus glorified his father – good! Ancestor worship is the core of Confucian society. The death on a cross is a bit melodramatic, but rebirth after three days is clearly a Buddhist influence.

So a holy sage who calls himself the son of heaven, wanders alone in the wilderness for forty days, glorifies his father, dies, and is reborn, well … why should *we* consider *that* foreign?

Besides, Hanaunim, the word Korean Christians use for god, is a word we have used for the divine being for thousands of years before the missionaries came. We are praising our own god and our own history when we praise Hanaunim. *[구궁]*

Yes, I would, thank you. Like this … as if the sleeve were long and heavy, and would normally fall forward. *[따]* In the west, you hardly ever see the meat before it is cooked. Here it is presented fresh, then sliced into thin pieces which are cooked to perfection in front of one's very own eyes. To the future? *[궁]* That's a bit general. To the reunification of Korea. *[구궁]* To the healing of our wounds and the joy of bringing families together. *[궁따]* Good. That will take at least … Two more bottles!!

I did my graduate studies in engineering, investigating stress in steel and alloys. Now I work in shipbuilding. *[엇모리 rhythmic cycle, softly]* Almost half of the world's new ships are made, each year, in South Korea. In America, they make less than one percent.

Once, while at a scientific conference in Chicago, I decided to see a baseball game. I like baseball. At one point all the people in the stadium were doing this with their arms, raising them up and down, singing a strange song. *[엇모리 rhythmic cycle loudly, then decrescendo]*

Thousands and thousands of people in unison, and I asked, what does it mean. An American colleague said: We are pretending to hold tomahawks, as if we are Indians. And I said, ah, you honour your ancestors this way and he laughed and said, no, no, not our ancestors, Indians, and then I remembered that the ancient spirits of your land are not the ancestors of the people who live there now. That was a hard thought for me to really grasp. We Koreans have lived here, on our land, for at least 5,000 years, probably much much longer! Double! 10,000! More! *[stop cycle]*

So you tell my sister, someone with roots that go beyond 10,000 years in this land, that she is not a Korean, even though you don't doubt for a second that you are an American, your ancestors having lived there for what, a hundred years? Two? And what did she do wrong? She considered new beliefs. There is nothing more Korean than that! Being open to new beliefs, understanding and integrating them, is part of the Korean tradition! It *is* our genius! *[구궁따따궁]*

The origin of Zen Buddhism in Japan is Seon Buddhism in Korea, which we adapted from Chang Buddhism in China. So why shouldn't we be open to the Christian influence of Europe and America? It's a question of using the right tool at the right time. *[궁따]*

We have an expression, *[엇모리 rhythmic cycle, mostly left hand (soft)]* three sages drinking from the same cup, meaning Lao T'zu, Confucius and Buddha. Our image is of them drinking and laughing together. Why not? While there may be disagreements, isn't it pleasant to discuss them? The air is mild, the breeze delightful, the conversation lively and engaged. We lean forward to hear what each of them says. Do you think Jesus can join them, or must he always drink alone?

You assume Jesus must always drink alone, don't you? *[휘모리 X3]*

Yes, I wouldn't mind. Another bottle!! Can only help.

People say that the singing of the natives in America sounds like ours, and that their dance looks like ours. Do you think that is just co-incidence? I don't. I think it is common roots still visible after ten thousand years. It was our ancestors who walked across the Bering Strait and spread throughout the Americas. Worth

thinking about. Soju. *[구궁]* Smooth Soju. Sweet Soju. *[구궁]*
Soju that dissolves our han and helps us to piss it out. *[구궁따]*

중중모리 *rhythmic cycle, forcefully*

You're not allowed pouring your own glass. I pour it for you.
That's how it works best. And when mine is empty, you fill it.
From those who can to those who need. Before my father died
he said things I don't think he told anyone else. I am sure he told
no-one else. He told his son, his first-born. *[stop cycle]* And it
meant something to him. And I carry it with me, I carry it, here,
in my heart. I carry it right here.

*The son, now quite drunk and lost in his own memories, wanders
unsteadily off the stage.*

**The musician plays a cello solo: the first movement of Bach's Suite
#1 in G major.**

THIRD MOVEMENT: SCHERZO

*The stage is emptied except for the musical instruments. A film
is projected. Focal length, sensitivity to light and speed of camera
movement are varied so that, most of the time, the image is
painterly and gestural. Certain sequences are looped, others
superimposed. Images both from the past and the future of the
performance are entangled, creating a visual exploration of tense.
There are many extreme close-ups joined by a visual formalism.*

*Images of the Korean daughter are interspersed and integrated into
the formal and gestural style of the film.*

*The sound begins with the Lord's Prayer in Korean, spoken softly by
the daughter. Her voice continues in snippets, but is overtaken by the
performer's recorded voice speaking as the daughter but in English.*

Daughter's Voice Over

I want to talk to you about how tense is used in the Lord's Prayer, and then I want to show you how it is used in the Apostle's Creed. The differences in how they use past, present and future, is important.

The Lord's Prayer starts with the collective possessive "our", our father, who *art* in heaven. That's the present tense, *art* in heaven, an enduring present.

This is followed by an expression of a desire ... *hallowed be* thy name, not hallowed is thy name, which would be a statement, or hallowed will be thy name, another statement, but *hallowed be* thy name, a current longing or present desire for something on the cusp of being, something imminent.

And then that desire for the imminent is repeated twice more, thy *kingdom come*, thy will *be done* ...

on earth as it *is* in heaven, meaning, what we desire on earth is what is present in heaven: there is a parallel between our desires on earth and what is *in* heaven ...

and that immediately is followed by three desires, all expressed in the present tense ...

give us this day our daily bread, that is, make available to us that which we need for our survival ... and *forgive* us, present tense, our debts ... but what is debt? It's a kind of imbalance, a fracture, between the past and the present, to be addressed in the future.

So there is a desire to not have this imbalance between the past and the present, our debt, that it be forgiven, right now, not in the future, but now ...

as *we* forgive *our* debtors, as we *forgive*, present action, all those from whom we expect retribution for the past ...

and *lead us not*, a present desire, lead us not into temptation.

But what is temptation? It's an illusion about the future which leads to a wrong action in the present …

but *deliver us*, a present desire, from evil …

and evil is now simple to define: it is lack of daily bread; it is carrying the imbalances of the past into the future; it is about illusions of the future which create wrong action in the present.

So the heaven we seek, through our present desires, is now visible: bread for all; forgiveness of the past; and a true, clear, without deceit, knowledge of what is in the present …

and so that which was imminent at the beginning of the prayer, is now present, is now with us.

For thine *is* the kingdom … present tense … the power and the glory, forever and ever … an enduring present … amen.

The tense structure, then, is this: present, present, present, present, present, present, present, present, present, present.

The past is never used. Not once, and the only time it is implied is that, in our debts, it be forgiven. Nor is there a future tense given, except that which is implied as imminent through the expression of our current desires.

Now let us turn to the Apostle's Creed, that obligatory statement necessary for membership in the church.

I believe … first person singular, present tense … in the Lord our God, maker of heaven and earth … and in Jesus Christ, his only son, our Lord, who was *conceived* by the Holy Ghost, past tense, and *born* of the Virgin Mary, past tense, *suffered* under Pontius Pilot, past tense, was *crucified*, past tense, *died*, past tense, and *buried*, past tense, he *descended* into hell, past tense, the third day he *rose*, past tense, he *ascended*, past tense, and *sitteth* on the right hand of the Lord, present tense, from whence he *shall come* to judge, future tense. I *believe*, present tense …

So, the tense structure is as follows: present, past, past, past, past, past, past, past, past, past, past, present, future, present

The structure emphasizes that which is important in the present is a belief in the certainty of a magical past: born of virgin, conceived by ghost, descendeth into hell, rose from the dead.

What was a religion of forgiveness, hope, and collective well-being through an understanding of the present and our desires within it, did, in its infancy, adopt a creed wedded to a magical past, focused on the certainty of death and future judgment.

So my question to you is simple, do we throw them both out, the Lord's Prayer and the Apostle's Creed, or do we celebrate the first as we let go of the latter?

FOURTH MOVEMENT: KÜT

The performer enters before the film ends, and taking on the persona of the American friend stands with one hand up as if holding a strap in a subway.

The film ends. Three slow strokes on the mok'tak

The American Friend

I take the subway to the temple. *[single stroke on mok'tak]* I've learned how to stand for an hour and a half with one arm up, holding the strap. *[single stroke]* I have begun to think of it as a challenge. *[single stroke]* I resent the empty seats which become available, as if they are tempting me to give into a weakness. *[slow strokes, rolled]*

But what is my weakness, really? Is it wanting to sit down, or is it this ridiculous pride of always wanting to prove a superior discipline?

So sometimes I sit, and sometimes I stand, depending on how I perceive the need of the moment, whether I should address my laziness or address my pride. You may think I am becoming more lazy because I sit more often, but I assure you that its only because I have finally realized that my pride is stubborn and infinite. *[little faster, clean strokes]*

I am sitting when a strange begging couple come through the car. *[little faster mok'tak, clean strokes]* They are tied together around their waists with a thick short cord. The man, in front, is blind, and holds a white cane in one hand and a small bowl for coins in the other. Behind him a woman, younger. She doesn't seem to have anything wrong with her, just a bit hunched, as if, perhaps, withdrawn into herself. Dangling off the thick rope looped around her waist is a small tape machine playing music. Blind beggars in the subway always play music. It announces their arrival and gives everyone time to fish around in their pockets for change. It's usually something conventionally beautiful like Amazing Grace, but the music these two are playing is traditional Korean music. *[stop mok'tak]*

It is odd, father and daughter, if in fact they are father and daughter, tied at the waist, the blind man leading the seeing woman as they inch forward, ever so slowly, through an indifferent subway car to the music of crashing cymbals, bells and wailing horns. *[ching stroke]*

I transfer at Chungmoro Station. *[ching stroke]* It is busy here. *[ching stroke]* Half of Seoul seems to pass through at any moment, and the city of Seoul is one of the great cities of our age. *[atmospheric ching strokes, later regularize]*

I am carried out of the car with the crowd, when suddenly I feel this urgency to move, to stand outside the current. There are large pillars in Chungmoro around which the crowd flows, like a high tide around a rock, and I, if I time this carefully, I can enter a small eddy on the lee side of that rock, stand with my back to it, unnoticed, immobile.

I do that. Then immediately concentrate on my breathing, trying to inhale and exhale simply. Not shallow, not rushed. Easy and deep. I achieve that. I feel proud of myself but then remember to let that feeling go. Let it go. Let all the thoughts come and go.

My eyes are open but I don't actually see, I hear, I enter into sound, become vulnerable to it, as it grows ever more vast and dense, *[regularize rhythm on ching]* an intricate knot of shifting rhythms of thousands of feet on the floor and numberless voices raised to be heard, an amazing sea of sound roaring in two directions at once as people simultaneously approach and depart, approach and depart, and each and every one of them filled with intention, purpose. *[stop ching]*

Let it go.

The floor sways. *[ching strokes regularized]* Is it only because I am trying to be so still that I feel it move? It is slight, but real. Why does it sway? Is it the rhythm of the people moving, or the trains arriving, or both? Or is it that the earth itself always trembles?

I become aware of the thoughts I am having. I notice their sequence. In the train of this thought, that thought, and behind this thought, that thought, ah! this thought leads to that thought and behind it this thought which leads ...

And all these trains of thought, they, too, filled with purpose, intention ... *[stop ching]*

The shame, the humiliation, the fear, the false pride, the arrogance ... let it go! *[ching stroke]*

The coolness from an air-conditioning vent wafts towards me, carrying the fragile scent of someone's perfume, ahh, sweet, and now a sour smell, perhaps the sweat of the same person, or another.

Let it go.

My eyes are still open and I begin to see more clearly all about me are people I have seen many times before, all from different stages of my life. Why is that? I recognize them by how they tilt their heads, shrug their shoulders, lean together, hold hands or guide their children.

Let it go.

I see myself among the approaching and departing, my many selves, and each insistent with intention, purpose.

Let it go.

On my face, now, the cool water of a childhood lake. My eyes open beneath the surface to look at my brother as he and I make faces under water the colour of weak tea.

I welcome that thought and let it go. Under the water we are bursting with stopped laughter.

I welcome that thought and let it go

Then the image, *[suspended ching, single strokes]* – why now? – of you reaching to the earth, your palm open, your thumbs each touching one finger and then a thousand arms holding a thousand cups as you face simultaneously in all directions *[speed up]*

even you, let it go …

Let go of the master, let go of the student, let go of the easy, let go of the difficult, there is no way if you don't let go of the way … *[climax of ching]*

Ssssh! *(spoken to the percussionist, ching slowly subside]*

Standing behind a pillar at Chungmoro Station I am shaken and awakened by the contempt and disdain within three words …

Shock and Awe. Who am I to remain silent about what we have become?

I can't let it go. A sense of responsibility holds the thought that will not let go. Shock and Awe. Have I lived a life of lies and murder only to allow the cycle again?

After swimming with us at dusk – the water oranges, golds, crimsons, ochres, even pale mauves and ethereal greens – the sunset reflected upon the breaking surface, my father would build a bonfire on the beach. The flames were beautiful as they leapt and fell. And we would gather around, shivering from the cool wet, spooked by the dark trees groaning in the raising wind behind us, we would gather and sing ... my brother, sister, parents and I, sing.

Kumbaya, He's Got the Whole World, The Wise Man Builds His House Upon The Rock ... and perhaps my favourite, yes:

(singing)   One more river, and that's the river of Jordan,
              one more river, there's one more river to cross,
              the animals came two by two,
              there's one more river to cross,
              the monkey and the kangaroo,
              there's one more river to cross

And then, at the end of the evening, if she were relaxed and happy, my mother might sing. I remember her high, soft voice – never quite in key – but such clarity, such conviction. She who brought warmth to my life was warmed by this song:

(singing)   The Lord's my shepherd, I'll not want;
              He makes me down to lie
              In pastures green; he leadeth me
              The quiet waters by.
              My soul he doth restore again,
              And me to walk doth make
              Within the paths of righteousness,
              E'en for his own name's sake.

I, the would-be Buddhist, [*slow mok'tak, softly rolled*] singing Christian songs drawn from the Hebrew psalms, my back against the pillar of Chungmoro Station as tides of many selves wash over the slightly swaying building, but the people are kind and pay no attention at all to the ageing white man singing, badly. [*stop mok'tak*]

Let it go. No shame.

I cannot return to that place, the fires of my youth, the songs of my youth, but neither can I entirely escape it, and because I can't leave, when I die I will be born again within this moment of responsibility.

Shock and Awe.

I dread the idea of being born to kill again. I dread knowing that many will be born as I was born and will live as I did live, to kill again. I want this suffering to end.

I do not want to weave the blanket of lies within which the tortured will be wrapped. I refuse to bury the slaughtered beneath six feet of lies. Again.

I hear a small hollow knocking within the roar.

Cello Solo: Last Movement, Hindemith Unaccompanied Sonata

The Mother

The mother has a thin white shawl over her shoulders. She has her feet and arms set as if she is playing golf on a putting green. She breaks her concentration and looks up.

My son says that the war between America and China has already begun. He says that the Americans have not only armed Taiwan, but they are re-arming Japan as well. It is hard for a Korean to watch the rearmament of Japan without ... second thoughts.

She appears to concentrate on the put

My son says that the invasion of Iraq and the coming bombing of Iran are directly relevant to the American-Chinese war.

She puts, watches the trajectory of the ball, which seems to shift abruptly, and then goes forward to pick it up.

He says that America can no longer compete in the international market, and must use force to control the supply of resources that keeps them rich. He says that his father told him that we will have to choose which side we are on.

She returns and places the ball back in place.

I wish my son had fewer answers and more questions. He is very successful, but there are times I think he is a weak man. But then, aren't we happy when our weaker children succeed? The stronger children, it is all right if they fail, they will persevere, and still find moments of enjoyment.

She again concentrates on her put.

My daughter is very strong. She can hold a contradiction in her mind without losing common sense. But I wish she had more confidence. I want her to leave here, to study or work abroad. I hope she will.

She puts, and again watches the trajectory of the ball, which also shifts abruptly, and goes forward to pick it up.

It is a strange conversation between her and the American stranger who stays with us. American Buddhism and Korean Christianity … is there an attraction, or are they repelled? Could there be a child from their union? Would it be an ugly baby? Maybe not.

She looks for a new place further upstage for a longer put

My husband died playing golf. Actually, it was on this course. He insisted that I come with him that day and I said I would as long as I could stay on the putting green. He wore his new shoes and his new jacket. He looked like a foreigner, which he liked. It made him feel successful.

I did then what I am doing now. When I play, I prefer when the ball doesn't go in the hole. I hit the ball …

She puts, and this time speaks as she watches its trajectory.

… it circles the rim, doesn't fall, but moves, deflected, naturally, in another direction. It is beautiful to watch.

I have just done that six times in a row. Six times. I think of it as six broken lines, yin lines, the receptive.

A year ago today I was standing right here when a man came quickly towards me in the harsh light, and I knew right away what he was going to tell me, before he spoke. Later, sitting in darkness, I listened to two of my husband's favourite recordings, the Bach and the Hindemith.

Today it is misty … and I think, just at the edge of the mist I can see you. You, who in a brutal age made yourself into the image of another to ensure our family would survive. What questions can I ask you now?

Will our son make a mistake burdened by anxiety? Will our daughter return after having lived abroad? For how long will I live alone, talking to you at odd moments? How steep is your climb of Pung-man-san-shun?

I remember … There is so much beauty in so many memories I hold, but I need not speak of them, not to you, for you, who are in the mist, you hold them. You hold them, too.

The Mother takes off her shawl which divides into two pieces, which she then uses as long white sleeves to beckon her dead husband. The Percussionist enters the space to join the mother. He begins to play and dance, finding the spirit of celebration. When he finishes, the Mother is seen kneeling at the front of the stage. She bows her head to the floor as the drumming figure disappears.

Key to Percussion Notation

The Daughter (hourglass drum [*changgo*] strokes)
기 (*ki* = tip of stick on rim), 닥 (*tak* = entire stick on rim), 기 (*ki* = tip of stick on drumhead), 닥 (*tak* = entire stick on drumhead)

The American Friend, The Son (barrel drum [*puk*] strokes)
구 (*ku* = grace note with left hand), 궁 (*kung* = stroke with left hand), 따 (*tta* = stick on top of drum [right hand]), 딱 (*ttak* = stick on top of drum, accented), 구 (*ku* = stroke with right hand), 궁 (*kung* = stick on right drumhead)

Rhythmic Patterns (*changdan*)
중모리 (chungmori = medium-speed 12/4 rhythm), 중중모리 (chungjungmori = faster-speed 12/4 rhythm), 엇모리 (ŏnmori = medium-speed 10/8 rhythm), 굿거리 (kukkŏri = medium-speed 12/4 rhythm), 이음새 (iŭmsae = faster-speed 12/8 rhythm), 삼채 (samch'ae = (faster-speed 12/8 rhythm), 빠른 갠지겐 (pparŭn kaenjigen = faster-speed 12/8 rhythm)

ACKNOWLEDGEMENTS

Historical Bliss (Gestus #3) was first produced at Studio Altaire in Montreal in 1983, directed by the author, performed by Harry Standjofski, costumes by Valerie Kaelin, music composed by Stephane Volet. It was remounted in 1984 at the D.B Clarke Theatre in Montreal, and later adapted into a film with the support of the National Film Board of Canada. A special thanks to Marie Slaight who, by supporting Studio Altaire, made the initial production possible.

Dog and Crow was first produced by The Necessary Angel Theatre at the Factory Theatre in Toronto in 1988, directed by Richard Rose, dramaturged by Don Kugler. Cast included Myron Natwick, Carole Galloway, Tony Nardi, Shirley Josephs, Ron White, Tanja Jacobs, Al Kozlik, Frank Pellegrino. It was performed again at the Prairie Theatre Exchange in Winnipeg, directed by the author. The translation into French by Louise Ringuet, *Cannis et Corvus*, was produced by the Conservatoire d'arts dramatique in Montreal. The script was developed with the help of Playwrights Workshop Montreal, The Necessary Angel Theatre, and the Banff Playwrights Colony.

The Consolation of Philosophy premiered in 1991 at the Toronto Music Gallery as an oratorio composed by Helen Hall, directed by Don Kugler, with Neil Munro as Boethius, Monique Mohica as Lady Philosophy, and a female chorus.

Freeport Texas was premiered by Sodium Glow Theatre in Vancouver at the Tinseltown Mall in 2005, directed by Olivia Delachanal, Assistant Director Miranda Huba, with Kristian Ayre, Nita Bowerman, Jennifer Cameron, Heather Doerksen, Lindsay Drummond, Stephanie Hayes, Nick Hunnings, Billy Marchenski, Frano Marsic and Tyler McClendon. It had development assistance through Playwrights Workshop and the National Arts Centre at the Magnetic North Festival in Ottawa, and independently through the American Conservatory Theatre in San Francisco.

Kareena had a public reading under the auspices of Teesri Dunya Theatre at Montreal Arts Interculturrels in Montreal. Developed with the help of Playwrights Workshop Montreal, the script was adapted into the screenplay, *Acts of Imagination*, a feature film set in Vancouver, directed by Carolyn Combs, which premiered at the Toronto International Film Festival in 2006. The theatre script was then rewritten.

Küt: Shock and Awe was first produced at Simon Fraser University, School for the Contemporary Arts, in 2006, performed by the author with Nathan Hesselnk as percussionist/cellist, directed by Kee Kook-Seo, with Maki Nagisa performing as the sister in the film directed by Carolyn Combs, stage managed by Ally Colclough. It was remounted with the same cast in a production by Craning Neck Theatre at the Waterfront Theatre in Vancouver, produced by Adriana Butz and Jeremy Waller, directed by Carey-Jo Hoffman, which production was invited to the World Theatre Festival held at the University of Puget Sound, Washington.

ABOUT THE AUTHOR

Michael Springate was born in 1952 in Rosemount, Montreal, the seventh of eight children to a British mother and a Canadian father. He studied painting and drawing at the Montreal Museum School of Fine Arts before turning to theatre. He founded The Painted Bird Ensemble, a collective that engaged in cross-disciplinary collective creations (*Scat, Fugue, Improvisations in Sonata Form #1, #2, The Gestii #1, #2, #3, #4,* and *Twelve Tones*). He was invited by Elizabeth Langley to join Concordia University as a sessional instructor, teaching performance within both the dance and theatres departments. He subsequently became Artistic Director of Playwrights Workshop Montreal, Prairie Theatre Exchange in Winnipeg, and Factory Theatre in Toronto. He became a lecturer, then a Visiting Professor, at Simon Fraser University, a Guest Researcher/ Lecturer at the May 18 Institute of Chonnam National University in Kwangju, South Korea, and Artistic Associate and Dramaturg at Full Circle: First Nations Performance, in Vancouver.

Plays he has written include *Historical Bliss, Twelve Tones, Dog and Crow, The Consolation of Philosophy, Kareena, Freeport Texas,* and *Küt: Shock and Awe.*

He wrote the screenplays for the feature films *Acts of Imagination,* which premiered at the Toronto International Film Festival in 2006, and *Bella Ciao!,* which premiered at the Whistler Film Festival in 2018, both directed by Carolyn Combs.

His first novel *The Beautiful West & The Beloved of God*, set in Montreal and Egypt in 2008, was published by Guernica Editions in 2014. The French translation by Jocelyne Doray, *L'engrenage des apparances,* was published by Les éditions Sémaphore in Montreal in 2017.

He is a founding member of Commercial Drive Productions, as well as the Vancouver Latin American Cultural Centre, and is an active member in the co-operative housing movement.